MIND REFRESHED

The Ancient Keys to Mental Health

The Explanation with Sam Kneller

From the smallest necessity to the highest religious abstraction, from the wheel to the skyscraper, everything we are and everything we have comes from one attribute of man - the function of his reasoning mind.

Ayn Rand – Russian writer

Anyone who stops learning is old, whether at twenty or eighty. Anyone who keeps learning stays young. The greatest thing in life is to keep your mind young.

Henry Ford

You cannot have a positive life and a negative mind.

Joyce Meyer – American writer

And be not conformed to this world: but be you transformed by the renewing of your mind, that you may prove what is that good, and acceptable, and perfect, will of God.

Apostle Paul – Romans 12:2

MIND REFRESHED

First edition. February 1, 2025.

Written by Sam Kneller.

For other distribution proposals, lectures, teaching, and speaking opportunities. Don't hesitate to get in touch with Sam Kneller at sam@theexplanation.com

Website: TheExplanation.com

Cataloguing-In-Publication (CIP)

Kneller, Sam.

Mind refreshed : the ancient keys to mental health/ Sam Kneller.-- France : The Explanation, c 2025.

275 pages: illustrations; cm.

Includes index.

Contents: Why God created humans on created earth– Why did God create humans?-- Earth's divine creation mystery– God's goal: care for all life– God's plan: humanity's true saga– Woman: the key to creation's tale– Why God allowed the serpent in Eden– Satan's Babylon to Christ's Jerusalem– Happy minds: mental health matters– God equipped humans to be kings and queens– Human consciousness: the breakthrough–Paranormal activity: real or not?-- Evolution debunked: human's neshama– Reasoning, the primary human quality– Purpose unveiled: a human trait– Why humans excel:

unique traits– ruach, role in humans– Two points: neshama and ruach– Bible ruach: Psychology 101– Bible Psychology for everyone, everywhere– Mental health begins in the womb– God's love heals non-believers– Bible psychology: mental health tips– Devine design: mental health blueprint– 21st century Proverbs commandments– Proverbs: humanity's guidebook– Mental health: 1000 therapy picks– Nurture and heal for mental health– Exercises to start beating anxiety– Bible Provers Method: sure relief– Purpose. Hit your bullseye– Bible Proverbs fix conduct issues– Reconnect friendships in the phone era– Workplace diligence: success guide– Consciousness: Science or Bible? – Wealth: is it life's sole purpose?-- Help kids follow instructions better!– Social bonding starts in babyhood– Teach organization: a lifelong gift.

ISBN: 978-2-9587628-8-9 9782958762889 (softcover)
978-2-9587628-9-6 9782958762896 (ebook)
978-2-487452-18-3 9782487452183 (hardcover)
978-2-487452-19-0 9782487452190 (audiobook)

1. Mental health-- Religious aspects-- Christianity. 2. Mental health. 3. Anxiety. 4. Theology. 5. Psychology, Religious. 6. Psychotherapy- Religious aspects. 6. Mind and body. 7. Consciousness. I. Title.

BT732.4 .K54 2025
248.8-ddc

About This Workbook

Mind Refreshed is the workbook follow-up to *Mind-Body Problem Solved*. *The Explanation* revealed, at length, WHY only theology has complete answers to the WHY, HOW, and WHAT of consciousness and mind.

https://TheExplanation.com/mind

Therefore, this workbook overviews those points. You can quickly brush up on the basics by consulting these chapters or videos: WHY theology (*Mind-Body Problem Solved* [1](Chapter 5, video), WHY the Bible [2](Chap. 6, video), WHY easily using Biblical Hebrew [3]Chap. 7, video) helps you grasp the God-intended meaning of Scripture and reach solutions to key personal and world issues.

Here's a 20-minute free mini-course, *Uncover the Mystery of Adam and Eve's Nakedness,* to see a vivid example of the no-fuss Biblical Hebrew method *The Explanation* uses throughout its writings.

https://TheExplanation.com/naked

The Bible plunges us into the Plan of God for all eight billion people on Earth. Part I of *Mind Refreshed* is a resume answering the big questions in life: WHY do the Universe, Earth, and humankind exist? How He created all humans to benefit from mental health, but we know babies are born sick, life hazards happen, and there are wars, tsunamis, and earthquakes. Chapter 6 explains WHY such events occur.

Then you'll see why the Bible is the mental health instruction manual for all people, believers and non-believers, no matter one's faith. Part IV explains God's love and concern for ALL humans.

Only when we assemble those answers can we see HOW consciousness and mind, as well as mental health, fit coherently into the picture. The follow-on is the recipe God exposes in His Word to nurture and heal mental health.

Unfortunately, religion has not seen the whole relationship between the Bible and mental health for all humankind. Now, you will receive complete insight into the *Bible Proverbs Method* to develop mental health in children, lessening by tons the problems assailing our young, adolescent, and adult generations today. Learn hands-on how to stop the hemorrhage and heal anxiety with this non-intrusive, holistic, valuable Biblical method.

In the book *Mind-Body Problem Solved*:

[1]Chap. 5: https://theexplanation.com/human-reasoning-no-explanation-for-the-mind/ **video**: https://youtu.be/NlRqMS-SZhE
[2]Chap. 6: https://theexplanation.com/where-full-definition-mind-body-consciousness/ **video**: https://youtu.be/B_FL_x9H960
[3]Chap. 7: https://theexplanation.com/fastest-bible-study-method-god-intended-meaning/ **video**: https://youtu.be/-a_7eMOrw8U

Table of Contents

Preface - Why Am I Writing This Book?

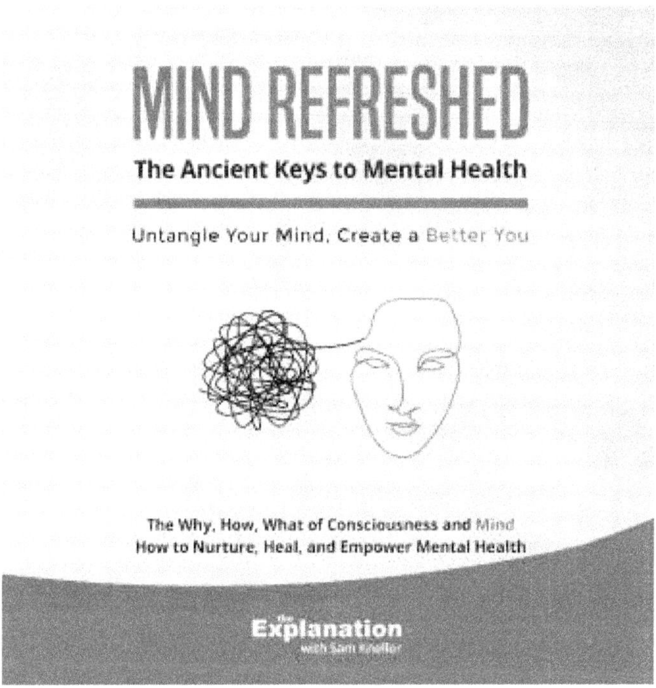

To reveal that God is interested in the well-being of every individual on the face of Earth. Whoever you are, there's a method to upgrade your life.

"Wow, Sam, you believe in God and a social God at that? Next, you'll tell us He has a well-thought-out plan for installing (you might say, *creating*) humans on Earth."

You took the words right out of my mouth. The capstone is that God gave each human consciousness and mind to function as we humans do to execute His purpose.

"Can you give evidence for that? You realize that most people, be they science, philosophy, or religion-based, would be dubious over such a bold claim."

Right again. That will be our quest at the beginning of this book. *The Explanation* will elaborate on the following topics to inspire you to upgrade your life.

- Why God created humans and placed them on Earth. How His purpose operates.
- Why humans possess consciousness and mind. Precisely how consciousness and mind function.
- Why human conduct is two-faced with good and evil. How this opposition should be handled.
- Why God is concerned with the welfare of all humans. How He gave humankind the tools to implement well-being.

Finally, we'll see what you can implement immediately to upgrade your life. The solution you will receive is your psychological compass, the *Bible Proverbs Method,* which will show you precisely how to prioritize your mind's options. It is your life guidance tool that shepherds you surely, at your tempo, toward your well-being and your place in society that God wants you to occupy, whether you believe in Him or not.

That is *Mind Refreshed.*

This psychological compass revolutionizes individuals' and society's approach to mental health, leading to a saner mental mindset with less anxiety and many other benefits like a better working environment, positive parenting, incisive critical thinking, collaborative management, and improved relationships. In short, the recipe to upgrade your life.

State of Mental Health Today

Here's why this information is essential and why its practical application is so vital.

The World Health Organization reports[1]

> In 2019, 1 in every 8 people, or 970 million people around the world, were living with a mental disorder, with anxiety and depressive disorders the most common. In 2020, the number of people living with anxiety and depressive disorders rose significantly because of the COVID-19 pandemic.
>
> Initial estimates show a 26% and 28% increase, respectively, for anxiety and major depressive disorders in just one year. While effective prevention and treatment options exist, most people with mental disorders do not have access to effective care. Many people also experience stigma, discrimination, and violations of human rights.

Here are some results of a survey performed by Eurobarometer[2] during June 2023.

> Forty-six percent of respondents have experienced an emotional or psychosocial problem, such as feeling depressed or anxious, in the past twelve months. 54% of respondents with a mental health issue have not received help from a professional. Most respondents replied that recent world events have influenced their mental health 'somewhat' (44%) or 'to a great extent' (18%).

The Role of Science

1. https://www.who.int/news-room/fact-sheets/detail/mental-disorders
2. https://europa.eu/eurobarometer/surveys/detail/3032

Scientific assistance to overcome the mental health crisis has been ongoing for 75 years[3] without reducing illness. Yes, they've alleviated certain contrary conditions, but overall, they've left psychiatrists and psychologists groping in the dark.

Here are a few fundamental queries about humanity tackled by Science. At best, some solutions are conjecture; at worst, there's no resolution. We don't hear much from Science on many issues, revealing how short they are in explaining everyday wonders, namely the origin of the big questions in life.

1. Earth is the only planet to support eight billion human lives and trillions of other life forms.
2. Earth has rain and harvests to provide food in due season. How do you explain that?
3. Why humans are on Earth.
4. Composition of humans: body, brain, consciousness, and mind.
5. How and why do humans and animals function differently?
6. The existence of interdependent genders for procreation.
7. Marriage and family: father, mother, and children.
8. The human capacity for doing both wrong and right.
9. Free will, reality or not?
10. Humanity has two significant challenges at this juncture in human history:
    a. A rulership crisis witnessed by collapsing government and environment.
    b. A social crisis witnessed by the disintegration of families and mental health.

Ten subjects are foundational for human existence, all of which have reached crisis proportions, and we're floundering in the dark to find

3. https://www.apa.org/education-career/training/national-institute-mental-health-transcript.pdf

the light at the end of the tunnel. *Mind Refreshed* will address all these issues and put you on the right track.

The Role of Religion

The second phenomenon is religion. It has failed to answer the big questions in life and provide viable, practical solutions. Spirituality exists and must be considered. *The Explanation* bases its teachings on God's Word, the Bible. A Key verse is Genesis 2:7. Previous verses lead to it, and subsequent verses expound on it. Genesis 2:7 is the Creation of the first human. Unfortunately, few recognize this turning point in universal history, but it is a momentous event akin to the awe of parents giving birth to their first child.

The Explanation claims that no one understands the extent of this miraculous development; the evidence is that no one can answer the following questions. When you do and assemble the pieces with the origins of the above ten issues, you'll understand God's Plan for humanity, what you're doing on Earth right now, and how to upgrade your life.

> **Genesis 2:7**
>
> And the LORD God formed man of the dust of the ground, and breathed into his nostrils the breath of life; and man became a living soul.

Here are ten unanswered queries about Genesis 2:7.

11. Who is the Lord? What is His relation to the Higher Power?

12. Why is *Lord* (Yahveh) singular and *God* (Elohim) plural?

13. What does *formed* mean? For instance, why doesn't it say created?

14. Why from the dust? What's the difference between dust and ground?

15. Why breathe into the nostrils? Why breathe at all? God could've used any method.

16. Did you know that *breathed* and *breath* are two totally different words in Hebrew? What does each mean? What is their relationship?

17. The Hebrew says the *breath of liveS*. It's plural. What's that all about? By the way, the *Tree of Life* is also the *Tree of LiveS*, plural.

18. Does *man* in Hebrew only refer to the masculine gender or something else?

19. What is a soul? That's the $1.000.000 question! Everybody talks about it, but for a definition, there's as much confusion as for the mind.

20. A living soul is singular. So why and how can a singular soul have a plural breath of liveS?

Mind Refreshed will address all twenty points and give you solid answers in a comprehensive framework. **Why** humankind exists, **how** humankind should function, and **what** each of us can do for our own and our community's well-being. You can upgrade your life, and *The Explanation* will give you the compass to do precisely that.

I. WHY God Created Humans on Created Earth

The reason powerful God created puny humans and placed them on the luscious planet Earth, which He specially built and designed for them.

1. Why Did God Create Humans?

Understanding ultimate Divine Purpose. God's Creation of humans is often scoffed at. Why would an intelligent God imagine such a contorted, seemingly contradictory idea, fact or fiction?

A Creation of humans by some *god* is almost ludicrous to many people in a 21st-century scientific world. Let's cut through the Gordian knot and go to the crux of the matter. *The Explanation* bases its understanding and teaching on the Bible, God's Word. The *Lord's prayer* starts with "Our Father Who is in heaven..." God is the Father of believers, and because He oversaw the Creation of humans, He is the Father of all humans, past, present, and future, who, by definition, are His sons and daughters (2 Corinthians 6:18).

Expanding God's Family is the Reason for the Creation of Humans

Father, son, and daughter; that's a family relationship. By the same token, according to the Words of the Father's Son, Christ, we are His brothers, sisters, and mothers.

Matthew 12: 46-50

> 46 While he [Christ] yet talked to the people, behold, his mother and his brethren stood without, desiring to speak with him.
>
> 47 Then one said to him, Behold, your mother and your brethren stand without, desiring to speak with you.
>
> 48 But he answered and said to him that told him, Who is my mother? and who are my brethren?
>
> 49 And he stretched forth his hand toward his disciples, and said, Behold my mother and my brethren!
>
> 50 For whosoever shall do the will of my *Father* which is in heaven, the same is my *brother*, and *sister*, and *mother*.

Understand the Divine Purpose. Christ Himself is the Son, as He refers to His Father. We are Christ's brothers, sisters, and mothers if we do the Father's will.

The big question is: In what institution do we find the father, mother, son, sister, and brother relationship? The family, of course. Nowhere else.

God created humans to be an integral part of His family. Please read that twice. Is God's Creation of humans to join His family corroborated elsewhere in the Bible? Yes.

- God is called our *Father* (Mat. 6:8-9).

- Jesus is also God and presently the only spirit-composed *Son* (Mat. 11:27).
- His Church is described as our *Mother* (Gal. 4:26).
- We are called His *children* (Rom. 8:16).
- In other words, His *sons* and *daughters* (2 Cor. 6:18).
- We are to be *brothers* of Christ, Who is the *Firstborn* (Rom. 8:29).
- He called those who do the will of God *brothers*, *sisters*, and *mothers* (Mark 3:35).
- The Apostle Paul refers to Jesus Christ and the Church as *husband* and *wife* (Eph. 5:22-23), who will be *married* at the Messiah's return (Rev. 19:7).
- The terms *begotten* (1 Peter 1:3) and *born* (John 1:13-14) are employed, referring to Christians.

Family relationships are one of the Bible's most underrated yet most prominent themes. It starts in Genesis 1, in the most awesome yet least understood manner. Let's investigate.

Genesis 1 States the Creation of Humans as Part of God's Family.

Genesis 1 refers to the Creation of fruit, herbs, seeds, fish, birds, creeping things, and beasts. An identical three-word clause describes each of these reproductive creations. Between Genesis 1:11 and 1:25, *after his kind* or *after their kind* repeats no less than ten times. Read these verses to refresh your mind. Go to UnlockBibleMeaning.com[1] to read them online. The frequent repetition of these words indicates a crucial reason the author wants you to recognize.

It is easy to understand the meaning of *after his kind* and *after their kind*. Peach trees grow peaches, and grape vines yield grapes. Trout

1. http://unlockbiblemeaning.com/

breed trout, beetles birth beetles, and giraffes engender giraffes; this refers to a species giving birth to identical offspring. There is nothing new under the sun except for the variety *within* a particular species that comes from cross-pollination, cross-breeding, or environmental adaptation. Yes, there's variety, but no, there's not, never has been, and never will be, a transformation of one species into another.

Genesis 1:25 says, "And God made the beast of the earth after his kind..." Monkeys can only engender monkeys, in all their varieties granted, but all are always only monkeys. God's Word emphasizes this ten times for all floras and faunas. The Bible indicates apes cannot give rise to prehistoric beings or humans, only other apes.

The Creation of Humans in the Image of God

Now read this résumé of Genesis 1 with the concept of *species* in mind.

> **Genesis 1:26-27**
>
> 26 And God said, Let us make man in our image, after our likeness...
>
> 27 So God created man in his own image, in the image of God created he him; male and female created he them.

Let *us* (plural, The two Eternal Beings Who are now the Father and Son[2]). Let us make *man*. The Hebrew word *adam* refers to all humans; this is clearly corroborated by verse 27, *male and female*.

Here's the question: What species are humans? The Creation of humans is after what kind?

Godkind. Yes, it sounds strange and unreal, but in one way, you're not surprised because of the prominent presence of multiple family

2. https://theexplanation.com/yahweh-elohim-inseparable-relationship/

references like father, mother, son, daughter, and children... that you are so familiar with. It's such a shame that you must wait for an *outsider*, *The Explanation*, to put two and two together.

Notice verse 28: God blessed them and told them to multiply and replenish the Earth. Put plainly, God gave His blessing, He married them, confirmed in Genesis 2:24, the man and woman become one flesh, and God said to have children, become parents, and practice parenting. The purpose of God's Creation of humans as male and female is to have interdependent genders to procreate. Learn the meaning of male (zachar)[3] and female (nekava)[4] in Hebrew; the two fit together sexually, like hand in glove[5].

We are human now, hence *humankind*, but the Creation of humans is after the *Godkind*. Humans have not realized their incredible potential. How can they? Many don't believe in God, and even in religious circles, the idea that humans are after Godkind is blasphemy. And yet it is right there in black-and-white in God's Word.

The Perpetuation of Humankind involves Family and Reproduction

God gave humankind the family institution[6] because He created us in His image. He's a family; that's why humans have families.

> **Ephesians 3:14-15**
>
> 14 For this cause I bow my knees to the *Father* (G3965) of our Lord Jesus Christ,

---

3. https://theexplanation.com/male-gender-its-significance-and-why-god-created-it/
4. https://theexplanation.com/female-gender-significance-why-god-created-it/
5. https://theexplanation.com/gender-equality-gender-inequality-or-gender-compatibility/
6. https://theexplanation.com/all-time-hidden-truth-elohim-god-is-a-family/

15 Of whom the whole family in heaven and earth is named,

We know God is our Father. Look at the implication of the Greek πατριά patria. It goes much further and includes lineage, family, and kindred[7].

John 1 reveals the bond humans can have with God. It, too, is a family relationship. Reading this chapter[8] will deepen your comprehension of this father-son (a generic statement, including father-daughter) family ties.

John 1:12-14

12 But as many as received him [Christ], to them gave he power to become the sons of God, even to them that believe on his name:

13 Which were *born*, not of blood, nor of the will of the flesh, nor of the will of man, but of God.

14 And the Word was made flesh, and dwelt among us, (and we beheld his glory, the glory as of the only *begotten* of the Father,) full of grace and truth.

Sons of God, *born* - by the will of God, *begotten* - referring to Yahveh Elohim[9], are all family terms.

Our Father, God's Plan is identical to that of human parents: to grow their children, His faulty humans, into believing, repentant members of His family.

7. https://theexplanation.com/all-time-hidden-truth-elohim-god-is-a-family/

8. https://theexplanation.com/yahweh-elohim-inseparable-relationship/

9. https://theexplanation.com/yahweh-elohim-inseparable-relationship/

In the Preface, we posed 20 unanswerable issues. With just one chapter, you understand why humans are on Earth (point 3), the Biblical origin of marriage, family, and interdependent genders (points 6 and 7), the Lord's relation to the Father (point 11), and that *adam* refers to both male and female genders (point 18),

In the next chapter, we'll see why Earth is such a luscious habitable planet.

PS In this Chapter and throughout this book, I use the terms *human*, *humankind*, and *humanity*, rather than *man* and *mankind* simply to be inclusive of women as indicated in Gen. 1:27. Men and women have different gender roles, as I explained in *Origin of Woman*[10]. However, each gender needs the other and is equally important for the human race in all aspects of life. Spiritually, men and women have an EQUAL opportunity before God, hence the use of *human* as inclusive of both men and women.

10. *https://theexplanation.com/woman*

2. Earth's Divine Creation Mystery

Decoding the breathtaking Divine Plan. The Creation of Earth. Our globe is not only habitable but, compared to other planets, it's luscious and bountiful, capable of furnishing 24 billion meals daily!

The Creation of Earth led to a blue water and green land sumptuous homestead for the present eight billion people. Correctly handling the resources would allow us to enjoy breakfast, lunch, and dinner daily.

To our knowledge, Earth is not only a planet that can support life but also a place where life blossoms and bristles with vibrance and opulence. You have to ask yourself why this is so. Is there a purpose behind this universal anomaly?

The Goal of the Creation of Humans

The Creation of Earth in all its splendor has an objective far beyond anything you or science fiction could imagine.

God created Earth as the space where His earthly family, His sons and daughters, would learn to grow and develop all their potential.

Here's God's definitive Promise to humankind during a future phase of His Plan, after Christ's Return to Earth, His Second Coming.

> **Revelation 5:9-10**
>
> 9 And they sung a new song, saying, You [Christ] are worthy to take the book, and to open the seals thereof: for you were slain, and have redeemed us to God by your blood out of every kindred, and tongue, and people, and nation;
>
> 10 And have made us to our God **kings** and **priests**: and we shall reign on the **earth**.

This scenario is your future, not only yours but also the billions from every nation who have lived, live, and will live on Earth. Our destiny is to be **Kings**, **Queens**, and **Priests** and rule on **Earth**. I've bolded that because general religion does not teach this fundamental truth. Our future is intimately bound to this planet. That's the reason for the Creation of Earth.

In the last chapter, we see God expanding His family[1]. What will be the occupation of this myriad of family members? It is not to stare at Him and only sing hymns of praise. We are to be Kings and Priests, Queens and Priests. Rulers and Teachers, Leaders and Law Instructors, Managers and Rulers. We will fill those unique positions—functions we will perform with Christ after His Return.

Do you take a man or woman and throw them into the role of King, Queen, or Priest? Of course not. We've all read about the rigorous and grueling training all descendants of royal families undergo in

1. https://theexplanation.com/gods-creation-of-humans-why-divine-purpose/

preparation for their future callings. Read about King Charles III[2] and Prince William[3]. His son, Prince George of Wales, will experience the same education.

These royal children have a goal. Similarly, God has set a reachable trajectory for each human, and the Creation of Earth is the training ground to accomplish this. If you train athletes, scientists, gardeners, or mechanics, you place them in the same environment as the one they'll occupy as professionals.

That training is *Mind Refreshed* to reach professional status.

The Goal of the Creation of Earth

Earth is luscious and bountiful, providing enough tools for EVERYONE to prepare.

Christianity is much more than *repent and be saved.* Yes, that's the start, but repenting and being saved is a personal, inward reflection and relationship with God.

Kings and Priests are outward, focused on serving others. That's what Christ came to do and what He calls us to do. The Creation of Earth is the practice ground for ALL humans now. God has given us the inventory to prepare for our future roles[4] in His Kingdom. Earth is an exquisite planet that produces our needs beyond anything we can imagine, and humans have unlimited imagination.

God spent almost six days preparing Earth before He created humans, just like we fashion a distinctive space for the arrival of a newborn baby. From the subdued lighting to the kiddie wallpaper, protective

2. https://content.time.com/time/subscriber/article/0,33009,900925-1,00.html

3. https://www.standard.co.uk/hp/front/the-royal-apprentice-prince-williams-training-programme-on-how-to-be-king-6846011.html

4. https://theexplanation.com/our-earth-soil-is-not-just-dirty-dirt-its-part-of-the-cosmic-puzzle/

crib, soft, well-equipped changing table, attention-grabbing mobiles, and soothing music, God did the identical for the Creation of Earth. Humans, even billions of them, have everything they need not only to survive but to thrive.

Creation of Earth, to Dominate and Subdue It

The second injunction God gave humans after telling them to socialize in a two-gender, children-bearing family relationship was to *dominate and subdue* the Earth. That is uplifting rulership and management.

> **Genesis 1:27-30**
>
> 27 So God created man in his own image, in the image of God created he him; male and female created he them.
>
> 28 And God blessed them, and God said ... replenish the earth, and subdue it: and have dominion over the fish of the sea, and over the fowl of the air, and over every living thing that moves on the earth.
>
> 29 And God said, Behold, I have given you every herb bearing seed, and every tree, in the which is the fruit of a tree ... to you it shall be for meat.
>
> 30 And to every beast ... fowl of the air, and to every thing that creeps upon the earth, wherein there is life ... every green herb for meat: and it was so.

Go and train to be directors and managers by using the resources: fish, fowl, animals, trees, worms, etc., that I've graciously provided for you to develop your talents. Create products and services to serve your fellow humans so you and all your families can thrive decently, healthily, and prosperously in your Godly-provided environment, Earth.

Read about this unbelievable, safe human place God supplied for our training in *Inventory of the Universe*[5] and the six days of the Creation of Earth in *Origin of the Universe*[6].

Respect Earth Like Apprentices Respect Their Resources and Tools

God has placed humans on Earth to exercise their kingly and priestly apprenticeships; they are management and teaching positions. The Apostle Paul said as much to members of the Church, but the principle is just as valid for all humankind. We have been given the world to *use* it properly.

> **1 Corinthians 7:29, 31**
>
> 29 But this I say, brethren, the time is short...
>
> 31 And they that *use* (G5530) this world, as not abusing it:
> for the fashion of this world passes away.

At *UnlockBibleMeaning.com*, check the deeper meaning of the Greek for *use* in Stong's Concordance. It means to handle, furnish, employ, and entreat.

The Creation of Earth was for human benefit, as I wrote in *Inventory of the Universe*[7].

> Our daily lives involve Earth when we work, sleep, eat, and play. Whether we're manufacturing or providing a service, sleeping in our bedrooms, camping in a yurt, cooking dinner

---

5. *https://theexplanation.com/inventory/read-all-the-content-of-inventory-of-the-universe-online/*

6. *https://theexplanation.com/read-content-origin-universe-online/*

7. *https://theexplanation.com/inventory/*

at home, feasting out, bowling, sailing, or studying, all our activities are directly related to our Earth.

God created humans and set them on Earth; He immersed them into a world of discovery. There is nothing more fascinating and stimulating than uncovering something new to us. Every day, in practically every field, we are unearthing new knowledge that should amaze you.

It should lead to the ultimate discovery: "The invisible things of him from the creation of the world are clearly seen, being understood by the things that are made, (the Creation of Earth) even his eternal power and Godhead" (Romans 1:20). That's another story; suffice to say now that the Creation of Earth is the best-prepared baby room ever for humans in their infant age.

In the Preface, we posed 20 unanswerable issues. This second chapter conveys the Biblical role of humanity in rulership on Earth and why our planet is so plentiful with resources and its harvests of food production (points 1, 2, and 10).

Working Labor, in All its Forms, is the Calling of All Humans

The Book of Ecclesiastes was written by the wise King Solomon at a particular moment in his life—today, we'd call it depression! Here, I want to focus on one of Solomon's essential recommendations.

Ecclesiastes 5:15-19

15 As he came forth of his mother's womb, naked shall he return to go as he came, and shall take nothing of his labour, which he may carry away in his hand.

> 18 Behold that which I have seen: it is good and comely for one to eat and to drink, and to *enjoy the good of all his labour* that he takes under the sun all the days of his life, which God gives him: for it is his portion.
>
> 19 Every man also to whom God has given riches and wealth, and has given him power to eat thereof, and to take his portion, and to rejoice in his labour; this is the gift of God.

Labor, in whatever our field of interest, be it manual or sedentary, is a primary element of our psychological equilibrium. The New Testament broaches management of Earth's resources with an additional application.

> **1 Timothy 6:17-19**
>
> 17 Charge them [Christians] that are *rich in this world*, that they be not highminded, nor trust in uncertain riches, but in the living God, who gives us richly all things to enjoy;
>
> 18 That they do good, that they be rich in good works, ready to distribute, willing to communicate;
>
> 19 Laying up in store for themselves a good foundation against the time to come, that they may lay hold on eternal life.

Humans, not just Christians, are supposed to *use* and *handle* the world with an outward-oriented perspective. There is absolutely nothing wrong with rich Christianity; we should use what's necessary for a decent life for us and our families. Excess riches are to be shared for the physical, mental, and spiritual benefit of all.

In the next chapter, we'll see what God is accomplishing by putting created humans on this created Earth.

3. God's Goal: Care for All Life

Humans caring for humans and Earth. Why? God's Goal is clear. First, He created a lavish Earth to provide all the vital inorganic minerals, organic trees, and food resources.

Second, He created humans and gave them two major injunctions: multiply your numbers through families and, therefore, **socialization**; manage the minerals and living organisms and, therefore, **rulership**.

Humans are preparing to be kings and priests, and we shall reign on the earth (Revelation 5:10). I want to remind you that Jesus is a King (He teaches rulership) and Priest (after the order of Melchizedek; priests teach socialization, Deuteronomy 17:11. Christ taught to love your neighbor). God's Goal is to prepare us to do what He is doing now.

God's Goal is to Beget Sons and Daughters

We are looking at God's Goal because this book is *Mind Refreshed.* We need to know WHY we should take that seriously and what to transform our minds into.

Genesis 5:1-4

1 This is the book of the generations of Adam. In the day that God created man, in the likeness of God made he him;

2 Male and female created he them; and blessed them, and called their name *Adam*, in the day when they were created.

3 And Adam lived an hundred and thirty years, and begat a son in his own likeness, after his image; and called his name Seth

4 And the days of Adam after he had begotten Seth were eight hundred years: and he begat sons and daughters.

These four verses give us the essence of God's Goal and teach us the meaning of the image and likeness of God. We have no difficulty in understanding verse 3, where Seth is the image of Adam. In English, we even have the term; he's the *spitting image of his father*; this refers to the outward features, the inward mindset, or both.

God's Goal is begetting (1 John 5:1, 15) sons and daughters precisely like Himself, after His image and likeness. I draw your attention to Adam in verse 2. The King James translators capitalized it, which is an error. Firstly, it's plural (*their* name, whereas Adam is the singular name of the first male). Secondly, *adam* refers to both the male and female genders. A better translation would be *human*; this shows the equality of males and females before God and why *The Explanation* says our destiny is to become Kings and Queens.

Chapter One of this book[1] details how God, Elohim, plural, is a Family with Two Beings now: the Father and the Son. The Mother is referred to in Genesis 2 with the Creation of Eve, who represents the Church (see *Origin of Woman*[2]), the cornerstone founder being Christ (that's why Eve was taken out of Adam). God's Goal is to beget sons and daughters precisely like Adam begat sons and daughters in Genesis 5:4 above.

God's Goal is Expanding His Family. Each Member, Male and Female, Must be in His Image

God gave us the family institution, which cares for humans, and a luscious Earth, which humans are to take care of, to develop His image.

Developing a family is a long-term experience: dating, courtship, engagement, marriage, birthing, parenting through childhood, adolescence, and young adulthood—a full-time process until their sons and daughters start their own cycle of familyhood.

1. God's Goal of Socialization

Throughout childhood and adolescence, children graduate, step by step, from dependence to independence. Parenting is caregiving, guiding, and supporting while their offspring gradually assert their autonomy. That's growing into the image of their parents, like father like son, like mother like daughter. This delicate balance requires patience and flexibility on the part of parents as they navigate the transition from dependence to autonomy.

Independence, but indeed not an island unto oneself; socialization is interdependence. Each son and daughter learns to integrate with society. Becoming social involves mastering practical skills and

1. https://theexplanation.com/gods-creation-of-humans-why-divine-purpose/

2. *https://theexplanation.com/read-all-the-content-of-origin-of-woman-online/*

developing emotional intelligence and social competence. Children learn to navigate relationships, regulate emotions, and empathize with others through interactions with parents, peers, and caregivers. This gradual socialization process requires years of experience and practice to internalize fully.

Proverbs 15:28

> The heart of the righteous ponders how to answer, but the mouth of the wicked pours out evil things.

This conversation is positive give-and-take. Christ went through this process in His family with His parents and brothers and sisters (Matthew 13:55). The reason parenting takes a lengthy twenty years reveals that God's Plan takes time, thousands of years, to give all humans, His sons and daughters, time to reach His Image, godly autonomy, and interdependence in His Family. This unique passage about Christ's youth is inserted here to show us Christ's and children's essential gradual growth period.

Luke 2:46-52

> 46 And it came to pass, that after three days they [Christ's parents] found him in the temple, sitting in the midst of the doctors, both hearing them, and asking them questions.
>
> 47 And all that heard him were astonished at his understanding and answers.
>
> 52 And Jesus increased in wisdom and stature, and in favour with God and man.

God established the family with a father, mother, brothers, and sisters to develop humans on an earthly level. That family is the physical representation of the image of His Family of Sons and Daughters, Kings and Priests, which He's in the middle of developing right now on Earth.

2. God's Goal of Rulership

God created Earth so humans could have *a room with toys to manage.* That's a bit tongue-in-cheek but not far from reality because as we mellow, we progress to more sophisticated objects in seasoned environments.

As individuals advance through life, their focus naturally shifts toward developing and managing (ruling) their careers; this entails acquiring the necessary knowledge, skills, and competencies to thrive academically and seize future professional opportunities. Such educational and vocational growth is an ongoing process that takes time and typically extends into early adulthood.

The ideal is to recognize the interconnectedness of humanity and the planet we inhabit; we are propelled to cultivate a sense of responsibility toward both. The development of personal careers should not be pursued at the expense of neglecting our fellow human beings or disregarding the well-being of Earth. Instead, it is essential to integrate a compassionate and sustainable approach into our professional endeavors; this is how individuals find purpose and meaning in their careers.

> **Mark 6:3**
>
> ... [referring to Christ] is this not the *carpenter*, the son of Mary...

The crowd knew Christ as a carpenter, *tekton*, in Greek, an artisan/craftsman, in particular, a carpenter, woodworker, or builder. That was

Christ's profession until the age of 30, how He managed/ruled His career. He was a builder in preparation for "I will *build* my *Church*," *ecclesia* in Greek, *assembly* (Matthew 16:18).

We multiply in families in the image of God's Family. We manage Earth in the image of God, who rules the Universe. Why do we care for other humans and the Earth? To reach God's Goal of growing into His image. One final point in the image of God.

God's Goal for Humans Interacting with Each Other and Earth Includes Ups and Downs

There is a time for joy and a time for suffering, a time for wellness and a time for pain. Life includes tests and trials. Kids scrape their knees and worse before they learn to walk and run. Scientists and technicians test rockets that blow up before developing a stable end product. A lot of basketballs miss the hoop before we build our skills.

We make mistakes with our families and friends in socialization, causing heartbreak. Similarly, we make mistakes in handling our personal and professional Earth resources, causing hardship. These trials and errors are a normal part of humans living on Earth.

Growing up to become autonomous adults is built through tests and trials. Children need opportunities to make decisions, solve problems, and learn from their mistakes. This iterative process requires time for experimentation and refinement. Parents play a crucial role in providing guidance and support while allowing children the freedom to explore and learn from their experiences.

James 1:2-4

2 ...count it all joy when you fall into divers temptations; (trials)

> 3 Knowing this, that the trying of your faith works patience.
>
> 4 But let patience have her perfect work, that you may be perfect (Sam: more mature) and entire, wanting nothing.

The basis of life is family and professional work in the image of God.

Learning from the trials and errors in our families and professions is the way to bring ourselves closer to God's Image. God's Goal is being accomplished right now in the lives of every human because He created and put us on a luscious Earth to experiment.

In the next chapter, we'll see the incredible result of why God placed humans on Earth.

4. God's Plan: Humanity's True Saga

The real story of humankind. God's Plan included a splendiferous Earth as a baby room for infant humans, the ideal place to learn to grow up.

Indeed, God gave humanity their marching orders to increase the population via family socialization and rulership over the planetary resources to benefit all its inhabitants.

This socialization and rulership is training to become Kings, Queens, and Priests and rule on Earth[1].

There are Two Ways to Rule:

1. God's Plan and Way are established in His Word, the Bible.
2. Anti-God's plan and way, i.e., all other ways, meaning according to the imagination of the human heart.

---

1. https://theexplanation.com/gods-creation-of-earth-why-decoding-divine-plan/

Humans are made in the image of God, Who is a Family and Ruler of the Universe. His ultimate goal in training humans as sons and daughters is for them to join Him and become integrated members of His Ruling Family.

Christ Prepared to be The Leader of Socialization and Rulership

Jesus Christ followed this schema of God's Plan. He came to Earth engendered by the Holy Spirit as the Son of God and the son of man via Mary, grew up learning socialization with His father, brothers, and sisters, and learning rulership/management via His building profession of carpentry. All this was before His unique Ministry of 3½ years, followed by His Crucifixion and Resurrection.

That preparation led to the Son of God, Christ, sitting on His Father's right hand.

> **Hebrews 12:2**
>
> Looking to Jesus the author and finisher of our faith; who for the joy that was set before him endured the cross, despising the shame, and is set down at the right hand of the throne of God [the Father]:

Yes, the Father has given His Son Rulership over humanity and Earth to prepare His brothers and sisters to join Him as Kings, Queens, and Priests to rule Earth with Him on His Return.

> **1 Corinthians 15:27-28**
>
> 27 For he [Father] has put all things under his [Christ] feet. But when he says, all things are put under him, it is manifest that he is excepted, which did put all things under him.

> 28 And when all things shall be subdued to him, then shall the Son also himself be subject to him that put all things under him, that God may be all in all.
>
> **Hebrews 2:17-18**
>
> 17 Wherefore in all things it behooved him [Christ] to be made like his brethren, that he might be a merciful and faithful high priest in things pertaining to God, to make reconciliation for the sins of the people.
>
> 18 For in that he himself has suffered being tempted, he is able to succour them that are tempted.

Christ alone is qualified and prepared to transform humans into leaders who can socialize and rule. The question is, how do you give everyone an equal opportunity to qualify? If you were an All-Powerful God trying to increase your family with the best possible sons and daughters, how would you go about it? Christ knows the way, the best way. We will elaborate on God's Plan to transform humans into Kings, Queens, and Priests who rule on Earth to bring real, everlasting peace to this planet.

The Original Mind Transformation Into Opposition of God's Plan

Let's go back about 6000 years. In the beginning, God created Earth (Chapter 2 of *Mind Refreshed*) and placed the created couple (Chap. 1) on it to grow their family and care for their homestead (Chap. 3). This was their training ground to learn to develop relationships and manage their belongings.

This family-oriented God wanted the couple close to Him so He could instruct and cherish them. He built a unique home headquarters, the protected Garden of Eden, where He placed them. Adam and Eve could cook and eat anything their eyes and stomachs craved except one tree.

Guess what? They were drawn to it, and after a convincing conversation with a stranger, they ate the forbidden fruit; this flip-flopped their reasoning capacity and minds forever; instead of incorporating God's Instructions, they wanted to follow their own thoughts and imaginations; this is corroborated in Romans.

> **Romans 1:21**
>
> Because that, when they knew God, they glorified him not as God, neither were thankful; but became vain in their imaginations, and their foolish heart was darkened.

God decided to let them follow their heart – or, in modern language, follow their inner voice or follow their intuition.

We must pause here and now and deeply grasp what happened with what led up to and followed the eating of the forbidden fruit. Adam and Eve rejected God (*glorified Him not*) and gave priority credence to their vain *imaginations*, resulting in a *darkened*, obscure, confused *heart*.

This reversal of reasoning is a crucial turning point in history. From this point onward, humans became jumbled in their thinking, introducing all sorts of ideas from voices they hear in their heads to dreams and, in particular, their overflowing imaginations and intuition.

Do Not Follow Your Heart, Inner Wisdom, Intuition, Voices, or the Like

Here's the first and probably the most critical lesson in this book. Do not follow anything or anyone that promotes looking into your heart for inner wisdom, intuition, voices, or the like; this is the opposite of knowing and glorifying God and looking into His Word. Here's Bible corroboration.

> **Isaiah 8:20**
>
> To the law and to the testimony (God's Word): if they speak not according to this word (the Bible *The Explanation* is quoting from), it is because there is no light in them.

No light means such godless teachers have darkened hearts and transform light into darkness.

> **2 Corinthians 11:13-15**
>
> 13 For such are false apostles, deceitful workers, transforming themselves into the apostles of Christ.
>
> 14 And no marvel; for Satan (the stranger in the Garden) himself is transformed into an angel of light.
>
> 15 Therefore it is no great thing if his ministers also be transformed as the ministers of righteousness; whose end shall be according to their works.

The Serpent transformed itself into an angel of light. Following such a transformation is DOWNgrading your life—that's what Adam and Eve did. We want to avoid this downslide at all costs; it is the cause of our individual and societal problems.

I know these are hard sayings, but if you want to know God's Plan for *Mind Refreshed* humans, you must understand the beginning, the first five minutes, what we must transform our minds from. From darkness, the voices in our heads, our intuition, and the imaginations of our hearts.

The Result of Rejecting God's Word, His Glory and Way

Romans 1:28

And even as they did not like to retain God in their knowledge, God gave them over to a *reprobate* (G96) mind, to do those things which are not convenient;

Adam and Eve and, subsequently, their descendants were no longer on God's Wavelength; they could not incorporate God's Spirituality into their reasoning process.

Humankind obliged their Creator God to teach them a lesson: You cannot disobey without consequences. He put them out of the Garden and padlocked the gate. Adam and Eve were now in the world with their jaded frame of mind, hiding from God in the trees.

G96

ἀδόκιμος adokimos ad-ok'-ee-mos; From G1 (as a negative particle) and G1384; unapproved that is rejected; by implication worthless (literally or morally):

KJV: - castaway, rejected, reprobate.

This rejection happened to Adam and Eve and, subsequently, all their descendants' minds.

2 Timothy 3:8

> Now as Jannes and Jambres withstood Moses, so do these also resist the truth: men of *corrupt* (G2704) minds, *reprobate* (G96) concerning the faith.
>
> **G2704**
>
> καταφθείρω kataphtheirō kat-af-thi'-ro; From G2596 and G5351; to spoil entirely that is (literally) to destroy; or (figuratively) to deprave
>
> KJV: - corrupt, utterly perish.

Read Romans 1:21-32 at UnlockBibleMeaning.com[2] to see their corrupt depravity. Then, compare it with our society today. The similitude is striking. Corrupt minds lead to depraved behavior.

The second critical lesson from this book is that God left humans with twisted minds. Humans wrongly reason that God is good and wouldn't let someone innocent suffer. God is good, but first, we are not innocent; we've rejected Him. Second, the reason He left people with corrupt minds is twofold.

He wants humans to realize that their imaginations, intuition, and hearts lead to destruction (the forbidden Tree of Knowledge of Good and Evil that leads to death). Secondly, only when humans have exhausted all possible experiments, inventions, and conceptions of their depraved minds will they come to their senses, realize they don't have the solutions, and turn to their Creator in all humility with a sincere *God help us*.

This answers point 8 in the Preface: Human capacity for doing both wrong and right.

---

2. https://UnlockBibleMeaning.com

5. Woman: The Key to Creation's Tale

The epic story of humanity leaked via the thrilling Creation of woman. Uncover the figurative meaning of the origin of woman.

After renewing Earth, God created the first human. He then planted the Garden in Eden and put the man in it. Only after that does God create the woman from the side of the man, who reacts by saying, *She was taken out of man*. The conclusion of Genesis 2 is the enigmatic statement: *They were both naked, the man and his wife, and were not ashamed*.

Have you ever wondered about these strange events and even more about their chronology? For instance, why didn't God create the woman and put the couple in the Garden together afterward? Why does God command the man ALONE to eat of the Tree of Life and not the Tree that leads to Death? It's so essential you'd think He'd address both the male and female about this crucial point, about which

Eve was deceived. Why does the woman come out of a man when both are in the image of God (Gen. 1:27)?

These verses are the first five minutes of God's plan for the story of humanity. The words, events, and sequences have figurative meanings. The major clue is, "And so it is written, The first man Adam was made a living soul; the last Adam was made a quickening spirit. The first man is of the earth, earthy: the second man is the Lord from heaven," 1 Corinthians 15:45, 47. The figurative story of humanity is a prophecy portraying the ultimate goal of humans.

The Meaning of the Creation of Woman Narrative in the Story of Humanity

Adam represents Christ. He is outside God's Garden, His Home and Headquarters, referred to as "In my Father's house are many mansions: if it were not so, I would have told you. I go to prepare a place for you," John 14:2. Through Christ's Crucifixion and Resurrection, He is the Firstborn, alone in God's House for now. The woman prophesies the *assembly of saints, the ecclesia* (Hebrews 12:22-23), which Christ founded on Pentecost when He was already in His Father's House (in the Garden) sitting at His right-hand side.

> **Hebrews 12:22-23**
>
> 22 You are come to mount Sion, and to the city of the living God, the heavenly Jerusalem, and to an innumerable company of angels,
>
> 23 To the general assembly and church of the firstborn...

The man leaving his family is Christ leaving His Father to marry His wife, the Lamb's bride (Revelation 21:9), to be one flesh, in a total spiritual union. Naked and not ashamed[1] in Hebrew means *clean-minded* and *not confused* in the Garden (see the free mini-course Uncover the Mystery of Adam and Eve's Nakedness[2]). *The Explanation* extensively describes each of these steps in *Origin of Woman*[3].

Story of Humanity in the Name *Eve*

Naming *Eve* in Genesis 3:20 presses home the *meaning of life*. This verse immediately follows after God pronounces the imminence of the man and woman's death. The question is, how does God's Plan continue? How can you save humans from death? Death, death, you shall SURELY die[4] (Gen. 2:17) if you eat of the forbidden Tree. How does God REDEEM them? Eve's name is associated with the story of REDEMPTION, how humans follow a trajectory from DEATH to LIFE.

> **Genesis 3:20**
>
> And Adam called his wife's name Eve; because she was the mother of all *living* (H2416).

The one-word *living* sums up the story of humanity. Only Biblical Hebrew reveals this narrative of humankind.

> **H2416**
>
> חַי chay khah'-ee; from H2421 (חָיָה); alive; hence, raw (flesh); fresh (plant, water, year), strong; also (as noun, especially in the feminine singular and masculine plural) life (or living thing), whether literally or figuratively:

1. https://theexplanation.com/creation-story-conclusion-naked-and-not-ashamed-thats-it/
2. https://theexplanation.com/naked
3. *https://theexplanation.com/read-all-the-content-of-origin-of-woman-online/*
4. https://theexplanation.com/life-and-death-major-issues/

KJV – + age, alive, appetite, (wild) beast, company, congregation, life(-time), live(-ly), living (creature, thing), maintenance, + merry, multitude, + (be) old, quick, raw, running, springing, troop.

H2421

חָיָה châyâh khaw-yaw'; a primitive root (compare H2331 (חָוָה), H2421 (חָיָה)); to live, whether literally or figuratively; causatively, to revive:

KJV – keep (leave, make) alive, × certainly, give (promise) life, (let, suffer to) live, nourish up, preserve (alive), quicken, recover, repair, restore (to life), revive, ([idiom] God) save (alive, life, lives), × surely, be whole.

The Story of Humanity in the Hebrew root of Eve, *LIFE*

The root of the name[5] *Eve* epitomizes the entirety of God's Intention for humanity, particularly following their eating of the forbidden fruit. Below, I have re-ordered the list of Strong's KJV translations to show you the progressive nature of the steps to take humans through their PHYSICAL and SPIRITUAL lifespan into ETERNAL life in God's Family. Let's arrange the translations below to reveal God's full Story of humanity. The following is a very brief overview of God's Plan. You might not know some steps, but they're all there; study (UnlockBibleMeaning.com[6]) and Bible corroboration make this evident.

1. **Give life**: Physical birth.
2. **Save alive, preserve alive**: During this lifetime, until we

5. https://theexplanation.com/master-hebrew-word-roots-basis-biblical-hebrew/

6. https://UnlockBibleMeaning.com

return to dust.

3. **Revive, make alive**: For example, the resurrection of the multitude in Ezekiel 37.
4. **Recover, repair, restore**: Healing of broken bodies and especially minds.
5. **Nourish up**: Role of the Church to spiritually feed the flock.
6. **Quicken**: Resurrection to eternal life.
7. **Be whole**: The ultimate goal of spiritual peace and prosperity in God's Family.

It is not, and never was, God's Intention to leave humans in a state of despair, abandonment, and even death despite humans hiding from their Maker in the trees in the Garden of Eden[7].

The Story of Humanity is the Restoration of the Relationship God had with Adam and Eve in the Beginning

Many Bible contexts witness this, and I leave that study up to you. One such passage is in Isaiah.

Isaiah 57:15-19

15 For thus says the high and lofty One that inhabits eternity, whose name is Holy; I dwell in the high and holy place, with him also that is of a contrite and humble spirit.

16 For I will not contend for ever, neither will I be always wroth: for the spirit should fail before me, and the souls which I have made.

7. https://theexplanation.com/light-to-dark-adam-eves-brutal-switch-from-open-to-closed-minds/

> 17 For the iniquity of his covetousness was I wroth, and smote him: I hid me, and was wroth, and he went on frowardly in the way of his heart.
>
> 18 I have seen his ways, and will heal him: I will lead him also, and *restore* (H7999 from Shalom) *comforts* (H5750 from Noah) to him and to his mourners.
>
> 19 I *create* (H1254 bara ... God has NOT YET FINISHED CREATION, He CONTINUES to CREATE) the fruit of the lips; Peace, peace to him that is far off, and to him that is near, says the Lord; and I will heal him.

God intends to *revive* (H2421) to bring about circumstances so that humankind learns to have a spirit of humility and repentance. He will heal, lead, restore, and comfort. All the implications are included in the meaning of the name *Eve*.

Notice why humanity upsets God: *going on frowardly in the way of his heart*. That's *reprobate*[8], the continued eating of the Tree of the Knowledge of Good and Evil, humankind making their own decisions regardless of God. Because of humanity's *iniquity of his covetousness,* God hides Himself from humans. This hiding refers to putting humans out of the Garden of Eden; we'll see why. But remember, God puts a veil between Himself and humanity because humans hid themselves from God first. Humankind obliged God to erect a *barrier,* as we shall understand in the following chapters.

As God says in verse 16, the barrier will fall, "I will not contend forever," but, in the meantime, there are thorny times because of man's iniquity and covetousness. This world is a time of sorrow in

8. *https://theexplanation.com/gods-plan-story-of-humankind-unbelievable-saga/*

socialization[9] and rulership[10]. We are thrashing and flailing around, applying our wisdom to find solutions.

Thankfully, verse 19 follows this calamity with the *creation* of *peace* and *healing* for those near and far, all of humankind—all of the living, of which Eve is the mother. In a nutshell, we have a summary of the whole puzzle climaxing in that Peace and Prosperity so desired but so distant from humankind.

The woman Eve in the story of humanity is much more than a name: she is the *life-giver*. Even more than just living, it should be a life of peace and physical and mental prosperity (3 John 1:2). Eve is the *knowledge that healing, restoration, and comfort are on the way* for ALL her children.

9. https://theexplanation.com/sorrow-the-meaning-for-the-woman-in-genesis-316/

10. https://theexplanation.com/genesis-319-sweat-of-your-brow-the-deep-meaning/

6. Why God Allowed the Serpent in Eden

The Garden of Eden is the closest place to paradise, the home of a loving God. Why would He allow an evil serpent to enter?

God refurbished Earth[1] and created humans[2], whom He placed in His HQ Garden of Eden, to rule and socialize[3]. Knowing only God, the couple was in a Godly state of mind[4]. However, one element in this paradisiac picture looks out of place: The Tree of the Knowledge of Good and Evil, which leads to death.

Why Were the Tree of Death and Evil Serpent in the Garden of Eden?

---

1. https://theexplanation.com/gods-creation-of-earth-why-decoding-divine-plan/
2. https://theexplanation.com/gods-creation-of-humans-why-divine-purpose/
3. https://theexplanation.com/gods-goal-humans-caring-for-humans-earth-why/
4. https://theexplanation.com/the-story-of-humanity-via-creation-of-woman/

Why would a *good* God plant an *evil* Tree in the midst of His Garden? Why would God tell Adam NOT to eat of this Tree? If God didn't want Adam and Eve to eat the fruit of that nauseous Tree, why plant it in front of them in the first place?

Is all of this a fictitious myth? Make-believe? The imaginations of ancient authors? These events are the first five minutes of the plot of humankind's story. If we cannot answer these questions with Bible-corroborated replies, we cannot correctly assemble the puzzle of why God placed humans on Earth.

To top it off, an incredible event took place. God allowed an evil Serpent into His Garden. The story says God threw Adam and Eve into the lion's den. That isn't an allegory, "Be sober, be vigilant; because your adversary the devil (the evil Serpent), as a roaring lion, walks about, seeking whom he may devour." 1 Peter 5:8. All hell broke loose in the Garden and continues to this day in our world.

In this short episode, numerous fundamental questions about God and humans cry out for solid Biblical answers. How *good* is God, considering He's at the origin of these events? He could've not planted the Tree of Good and Evil. He could've prevented this evil Serpent from breaking into the Garden. By the way, God could've simply put an end to the Serpent; why didn't He? Why did He allow the couple to choose whether or not to eat from the forbidden Tree? Did God know ahead of time they'd eat the forbidden fruit?

The outcome was that Adam and Eve's decision-making abilities drastically altered their reasoning capacity. Instead of enjoying the openness and beauty of the Garden, they hid from their Creator in the obscurity of a clump of trees. Their mental stability took a turn for the worse. That's why we've got to go back to the beginning and answer such fundamental questions.

Our Mental Health is at Stake

The Explanation wrote *Mind-Body Problem Solved* because Science, Philosophy, and Religion don't know what consciousness and mind are, how they work, or why we have them. All the answers are in Genesis 2:7, precisely the breath (neshama-consciousness) of life and the spirit in man (Job 32:8, Zechariah 12:1), the ruach-mind. This book, *Mind Refreshed*, is the sequel explaining WHY God gave us consciousness and mind, HOW they work, and WHAT each of us can do to build (in our children), maintain, and heal broken mental health.

These first events in Genesis are vital for comprehension. Unfortunately, the translations do not do the story justice. *Naked and not ashamed* (Genesis 2:25) mean precisely that, but that physical statement hides the more critical state of their minds[5]. Adam and Eve were *mentally stable and not confused.* After spending the seventh day with God (Genesis 2:3)[6], they understood the essential path to follow.

Good and Evil Present to Oblige Humans to Choose

Here are the answers to the above questions and, more relevantly, the purpose of God setting this scenario in motion. Firstly, God allows wrong-doing (the Tree of Death and the Evil Serpent) to be in our midst so we can make choices, hopefully, the right ones. However, the choice of our behavior is ours; humans have free will, and we must choose. There must be two clear directions to choose: God's Way and the evil Serpent's way.

Choice is a Bible theme from Genesis to Revelation. God always encourages humans to make the right choice (Deuteronomy 30:19) but never decides for us. Furthermore, and this will surprise many, He

5. https://theexplanation.com/creation-story-conclusion-naked-and-not-ashamed-thats-it/

6. https://theexplanation.com/god-pursued-his-work-resting-with-adam-and-eve-whom-he-created-to-make/

does NOT know our choice. If God knows what our decision is ahead of time, then we do NOT have free choice. Yes, God can and does know certain events and ultimate decisions ahead of time, but He is NOT omniscient regarding your or my spiritual future. Again, if that were the case, there would be no need for trials via the evil Serpent. Be careful of teachings to the contrary.

Here's a Bible verse that clearly reveals this and another critical principle. Yes, the verse applies to a spiritually converted person, but the underlying lesson applies to Adam and Eve and every human who has walked the face of this Earth.

> **1 Corinthians 5:5**
>
> To deliver such an one to Satan for the destruction of the flesh, that the spirit may be saved in the day of the Lord Jesus.

Many might think that a loving God would keep a sinner close to Him because that's the best way to help them. Not so, God expulses opposers from His presence; that's what He did with Adam and Eve in the Garden, NOT to condemn them, BUT so, just like this individual in the Church at Corinth, they LEARN THE MOST IMPORTANT LIFE LESSON: YOU MUST MAKE THE RIGHT CHOICE. And that choice is to align yourself with God's Way.

Satan, the evil Serpent, is a tool to help us realize *sin does not pay*. Because of humankind's depraved mind, God is allowing us to learn through war, sickness, sorrow, and anxiety so that we can come to our senses and change our decision pathways. God is giving everyone, at all times, whether converted or not, the choice to follow the right way.

God's Purpose for Humanity Focuses on the Long-Term

Humanity focuses on the short term! And in 2025, the short term is getting shorter and shorter with attention spans and fulfilling our pleasures. Express delivery of goods, food, etc., faster internet to deliver often unverified information, and social media are all designed to satisfy our immediate cravings. Carrying mobile phones is symptomatic of this wayward trend of our *I must have it now* society.

God's Plan is long-term. He removed the man from the Church at Corinth so he could ultimately be saved. God accepts the temporary destruction of the flesh so that humans can transform their minds and upgrade their lives permanently. God is good and knows how best to deal with all humans for their long-term success. The point is He planted the Tree of Good and Evil and allowed the evil Serpent to penetrate the Garden, just as He allows wars, famine, and sickness for the long-term benefit. Understand that God prefers this evil not exist and shows us how to avoid it, as we'll see, but He permits it for our ultimate good.

Two Sources and Two Areas of *Sorrow* which is Anxiety

Starting immediately after Adam and Eve's disobedience, the **first source of sorrow is ourselves**; God predicts sorrow in the two major areas of our lives: family (socialization) and professional and other occupations (rulership).

> **Genesis 3:15-17**
>
> 15 And I will put enmity between you [Serpent] and the woman, and between your seed and her seed; it shall bruise your head, and you shalt bruise his heel.
>
> 16 To the woman he said, I will greatly multiply your *sorrow* (H6093), and your conception; in *sorrow* (H6089) you shall

bring forth children; and your desire shall be to your husband, and he shall rule over you (socialization).

17 And to Adam he said, Because you have hearkened to the voice of your wife, and have eaten of the tree, of which I commanded you, saying, You shall not eat of it: cursed is the ground for your sake; in *sorrow* (H6093) shall you eat of it all the days of your life (rulership);

Sorrow is a universal sentiment. Both men and women are vessels of this sorrow. Here's the meaning of this Biblical Hebrew word.

H6093

עִצָּבוֹן ‘itstsâbôwn its-tsaw-bone'; from H6087 (עָצַב); worrisomeness, i.e. labor or pain:

KJV - sorrow, toil.

H6087

עָצַב ‘âtsab aw-tsab'; a primitive root; properly, to carve, i.e. fabricate or fashion; hence (in a poor sense) to worry, pain or anger:

KJV - displease, grieve, hurt, make, be sorry, vex, worship, wrest.

Worry, pain, vexation, displeasure, grief, and hurt are all synonyms of anxiety, today's number one mental health problem worldwide. In the Western world and significant parts of Asia, we have all the gadgets you'd think to make our lives satisfying, yet we're empty; we've lost the contented feeling of fulfillment. Peace of mind has dissipated like smoke in the air.

The Second Source of Sorrow is The Evil Serpent.

> **Genesis 3:15**
>
> And I will put enmity between you [the evil Serpent] and the woman, and between your seed and her seed [her descendants, all humanity]; it shall bruise your head, and you (the evil Serpent) shall bruise his heel (cause anxiety).

The evil Serpent is a cause of destruction, as we saw regarding the man in the Church in Corinth. But the bottom line is the man's wrong socialization is the cause of his pain and anxiety. Eliminating wrong practices, thoughts, and pre or misconceptions relieves anxiety. That's the crux of *Mind Refreshed.*

7. Satan's Babylon to Christ's Jerusalem

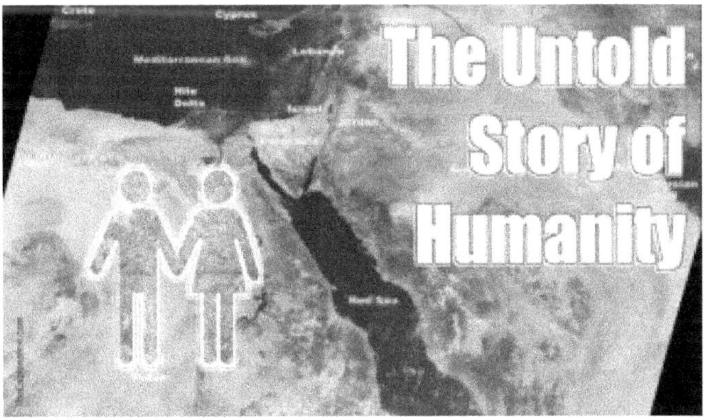

Human spiritual story. Are we ready to follow the way from Babylon to Jerusalem? To transform our minds and change citizenship?

God put humans on Earth to learn family relationships and rulership of Earth's resources. Today, the family institution and the environment are in a free-fall plunge, causing untold sorrow[1]. Will we stop this hemorrhage, turn it around, and heal the wounds?

The Bible explains why we're in this mess and reveals God's Plan to bring peace and prosperity to all humankind. This long-term endeavor revolves around one point: transforming everybody's mind. Let's discover that fascinating narrative via two cities, Jerusalem and Babylon, and three consecutive timeframes, 6000 years, 1000 years, and 100 years.

We discussed the Serpent's role[2]. Remember, it's a tool God uses to show us there are two distinct ways: God's and Satan's. These two life

1. https://theexplanation.com/why-good-god-allow-evil-serpent-garden-of-eden/

paths are symbolized throughout the Bible by light and dark, the Tree of Life and the Tree of Death. This chapter highlights God's Plan via Jerusalem and Babylon; the former belongs to God, and the latter to the Serpent.

First Period: Satan's Babylon, 6000 Years of Deception

The Bible story starts and ends in a specific location, God's World-ruling Headquarters. The four rivers issuing from its midst identify the Garden of Eden as the site of Jerusalem. "And a river went out of Eden to water the garden; and from thence it was parted, and became into four heads," Genesis 4:10.

Compare this with Revelation 22:1-2, a description of New Jerusalem. "And he shewed me a pure river of water of life, clear as crystal, proceeding out of the throne of God and of the Lamb... and on either side of the river, was there the tree of life, which bare fruit and the leaves of the tree were for the healing of the nations (the world)."

Our story starts in the Garden, where the Serpent twists Eve's mind into deception.

> **1 Timothy 2:14**
>
> And Adam was not *deceived*, but the woman being *deceived* was in the transgression.
>
> **2 Timothy 3:13**
>
> But evil men and seducers shall wax worse and worse, *deceiving* (G4105), and being *deceived* (G4105).
>
> **Revelation 12:9**

---

2. https://theexplanation.com/why-good-god-allow-evil-serpent-garden-of-eden/

> And the great dragon was cast out, that old serpent, called the Devil, and Satan, which *deceives* (G4105) the whole world: he was cast out into the earth, and his angels were cast out with him.

The Serpent is the behind-the-scenes deceiver of the whole Earth, transferring it from Eden/Jerusalem to Babylon.

Note that this deception will wax worse and worse. Our post-modern, social media, fake news, AI, propaganda society fits that description to a tee. Let's pinpoint the target: the mind. That's where this dark, sly battle is taking place. It's mind control at the most profound level unbeknown to them who are the objects of this morally bankrupt strategy. Adam and Eve's degenerate minds were the reason God expelled them from the Jerusalem Garden into the outskirts of Eden.

> **G4105**
>
> πλανάω planaō plan-ah'-o; From G4106; to (properly cause to) *roam* (from safety truth or virtue):
>
> KJV - go astray, deceive, err, seduce, *wander*, be out of the way.
>
> **G4106**
>
> πλάνη planē plan'-ay; Feminine of G4108 (as abstraction); objectively fraudulence; subjectively a *straying* from orthodoxy or piety:
>
> KJV - deceit, to deceive, delusion, error.

Satan caused Adam and Eve's makeover; they *strayed* and became *wanderers*. Remember that after murdering his brother, Cain was expelled from Eden into the *land of Nod*.

Genesis 4:16

And Cain went out from the presence of the LORD, and dwelt in the land of *Nod* (H5113), on the east of Eden.

H5113

Nôwd נוֹד node; the same as H5112 (נוֹד) lemma נוֹד extra dagesh, corrected to נוֹד; vagrancy; Nod, the land of Cain:

KJV - Nod.

H5112

nôwd נוֹד node; (only defective נֹד); from H5110 (נוּד); exile:

KJV - wandering.

H5110

nûwd נוּד nood; a primitive root; to nod, i.e. waver; figuratively, to wander, flee, disappear; also (from shaking the head in sympathy), to console, deplore, or (from tossing the head in scorn) taunt:

KJV - bemoan, flee, get, mourn, make to move, take pity, remove, shake, skip for joy, be *sorry*, vagabond, way, *wandering*.

Nod is the *Land of Wandering and sorrow, East of Eden* (i.e. Babylon). It is not just walking and exploring; it's essentially figurative, meaning a *wandering* mind, a *deceived* mind. Once out of the Garden and Eden, you're roaming around in a quicksand minefield of conflicting hypotheses in science, philosophy, intuition, and religion. Later, Nimrod builds the Tower of Babel, the epitome of the Serpent who reached up to usurp God's Throne. Then, about 600 BC, we find the remains of Israel, the tribes of Judah, Levi, and Benjamin, being taken into captivity, extracted from Jerusalem, and transplanted in the region of Babylon.

Babylon was a vibrant and robust city that sat astride the Euphrates River. It was one of the wonders of antiquity; today, its ruins are about 80 km south of Bagdad, near the modern city of Al-Hillah in Iraq. Here are both the royalty and depravity of Babylon.

Revelation 18:1-5

1 I will shew to you the judgment of the great whore that sits upon many waters:

2 With whom the kings of the earth have committed fornication, and the inhabitants of the earth have been made drunk with the wine of her fornication.

4 And the woman was arrayed in purple and scarlet colour, and decked with gold and precious stones and pearls, having a golden cup in her hand full of abominations and filthiness of her fornication: (Sam: royal riches of incredible magnitude, but very depraved)

5 And upon her forehead was a name written, MYSTERY, BABYLON THE GREAT, THE MOTHER OF HARLOTS AND ABOMINATIONS OF THE EARTH.

Babylon is the Emperor, Kaiser, Ceasar, the mighty overlord, Satan misusing science, philosophy, intuition, and religion to plunge the world into abominations.

First Period: God's Jerusalem of Firstborn

During this 6000-year timeframe, there are a few bright spots. Abraham was the father of the faithful whom God called out of the East to return to Jerusalem. Then there's Joseph, who ends up in Egypt, a Biblical parallel to Babylon. There's Moses, who leads the tribes out, and Joshua, who again installs them in Eden (figuratively), the land of milk and honey. There's King David, and especially the arrival of Jesus, His disciples, and the establishment of the Church, the Assembly of God.

> **Hebrews 12:22-23**
>
> 22 But you are come to mount Sion, and to the city of the living God, the heavenly Jerusalem, and to an innumerable company of angels,
>
> 23 To the general assembly and church of the firstborn,

These are the small minority who, with God's Help, come out of Babylon, out of this world, and return to Jerusalem/Eden. This first period culminates with Christ's Return and Armageddon, the Kings of the East (Babylon), and the world battling Christ for Jerusalem.

Second Period: 1000 Years of Godly Rule from Jerusalem

Babylon, the whore is vanquished, and the Serpent is restrained in a pit, unable to deceive the nations for 1000 years (Rev. 20). It's the elimination of all opposition to God.

Zechariah 14: 8-9, 16

8 And it shall be in that day, that living waters shall go out from Jerusalem; half of them toward the former sea, and half of them toward the hinder sea: in summer and in winter shall it be.

9 And the LORD shall be king over all the earth: in that day shall there be one LORD, and his name one.

16 And it shall come to pass, that every one that is left of all the nations which came against Jerusalem (Armageddon) shall even go up from year to year to worship the King, the LORD of hosts, and to keep the feast of tabernacles.

Isaiah 2:3 ... and he [God] will teach us of his ways, and we will walk in his paths: for out of Zion shall go forth the law, and the word of the LORD from Jerusalem.

Notice the receptive minds. These people know that "the knowledge of God is the basis of wisdom, (Pro. 1:7.) They transform their minds.

This Millenial reign is when all those who prepared during the 6000 years will reign as SPIRIT Kings, Queens, and Priests on EARTH (1 Corinthians 15:52-53). They will be the private teachers of the multitude of survivors of Armageddon after the end of the first period.

Much can be written about the Millennium. Retain that it is the Government of God from Jerusalem, with God's faithful teachers spreading His ways worldwide. This second period reveals the positive results of applying God's Jerusalem Truth as opposed to the first 6000-year period of applying the Serpent's Babylonian deception. The results will be evident when comparing both periods.

Third Period: Probably 100 years, the Resurrection of All People Who Never Heard God's Truth

Here's where one of the most significant religious Babylonian deceptions is replaced by Jerusalsem's Truth. People who never knew God during the first 6000-year period are NOT lost. That would be unfair of a just and loving God. He gives everyone an equal chance to be called, transform their minds, accept Christ as Saviour, and prepare for their roles as Kings, Queens, and Priests.

> **Revelation 20:5, 13**
>
> 5 But the rest of the dead lived not again until the thousand years were finished. This is the first resurrection.
>
> 13 And the sea gave up the dead which were in it; and death and hell delivered up the dead which were in them: and they were judged every man according to their works.

All the dead from the 6000-year first period return to a healthy life in a Godly, Jerusalem world. They'll be taught God's Ways and compare this Jerusalem society with their former Babylonian society. They'll have time to grow spiritually and make the right choices; God will judge them according to their works after their resurrection when they know God.

Babylon and all opposition will meet a definitive end, and New Jerusalem will reign. We can transform our minds now and prepare for a return to the Garden of Eden, the New Jerusalem.

8. Happy Minds: Mental Health Matters

Happy is he (and she) seems to be a familiar, almost bland, if not weak statement. Not so. Why your mental health is at stake

"Happy is he..." unlocks the key to why God wants you to have your *Mind Refreshed*. So far, we've seen seven steps.

1. God created humans[1].
2. God created Earth[2]
3. God put humans on Earth[3] to care for one another (socialization—it's somewhat of a mess today) and master Earth's resources (rulership—we're plundering it today).
4. God allowed the Serpent and sin into the Garden[4] because all

---

1. https://theexplanation.com/gods-creation-of-humans-why-divine-purpose/
2. https://theexplanation.com/gods-creation-of-earth-why-decoding-divine-plan/
3. https://theexplanation.com/gods-goal-humans-caring-for-humans-earth-why/
4. https://theexplanation.com/why-good-god-allow-evil-serpent-garden-of-eden/

humans must choose the right or wrong path. God does not make that choice; He gave us free will to make it ourselves. We must exercise it.

5. Humans made the wrong choice[5], and God turned them over to a reprobate mind. Today, humans apply their wisdom to solve problems which, instead, compound themselves.
6. After their sin, Adam named Eve, which means restore and live[6]. In other words, God plans to retrieve all humans from their downfall.
7. This spiritual uphill pathway means bringing them out of Babylon and back to Jerusalem[7], the Garden of Eden. There are three periods to accomplish this for all humans.

The world is now in Babylon. This chapter is about *happy is he*, even in Babylon. We have free choice to live a physically and mentally prosperous and healthy life.

Happy is He is Not Compatible with Living in Babylon

Let's paint a picture of our Babylonian society. It is in hard straights with socialization. Look at broken families and broken children. We don't have the space here to elaborate. There's plenty of good, but there seems to be more bad. Let's not be duped; there's a downslide into more disrespect, rudeness, and incivility, which leads to more delinquency, despondency, escapism in alcohol, more complex and harder drugs, with more anxiety and depression.

The question is not, why does God allow this? We've answered that; He's turned humans over to their reprobate, think-they-know-better minds to take socialization and rulership into their own hands.

---

5. https://theexplanation.com/gods-plan-story-of-humankind-unbelievable-saga/
6. https://theexplanation.com/the-story-of-humanity-via-creation-of-woman/
7. https://theexplanation.com/human-spiritual-story-from-babylon-to-jerusalem/

The real question, and the reason for this book, is: In Babylon, can humans lead a happy, decent life? Yes. Did God provide a way of life IN Babylon for humans to survive and thrive? Yes. That way is not necessarily easy, but God equipped Adam and Eve with that *happy is he* way IN the Garden of Eden just before He expelled them, just like you'd equip your brother or sister with a parachute BEFORE you *helped them out of a plane* for a skydive.

What is the parachute God gave each of us?

Proverbs 29:18

> Where there is no vision, the people perish: but he that keeps the law, happy is he.

The first vital point I want you to grasp is the audience to whom this, and indeed, all the Proverbs are addressed and with whom they are concerned: *the people, he*. In other words, these are not converted or even spiritual people. They are Mr. and Mrs everybody, whether they read the Bible or not. Everyone is concerned. We shall return to this capital point when we go into more detail about Proverbs. Just keep in mind these injunctions are for the general public, which is gulping down Prozac and anything else they feel might alleviate their mental illness.

Deceitful Vision

This verse describes Babylon and the antidote. *Happy is he* while living in this world when they *keep the law*... we shall see what's involved. The first part of this verse portrays today's shortsightedness, decisions based on upcoming elections, immediate needs, and fast-buck financial gains. Lack of purpose causes anxiety. Here's the meaning of *vision*.

H2377

> חָזוֹן châzôwn khaw-zone'; from H2372 (חָזָה); a sight (mentally), i.e. a dream, revelation, or oracle:
>
> KJV - vision.
>
> **H2372**
>
> חָזָה châzâh khaw-zaw'; a primitive root; to gaze at; mentally to perceive, contemplate (with pleasure); specifically, to have a vision of:
>
> KJV - behold, look, prophesy, provide, see.

Happy is he and *she* who have vision, can contemplate the future with pleasure, and have a mental perception of being provided for, in other words, leading a fulfilled life. Consider how many people are in that situation today!

Notice the seemingly out-of-place translation prophesy. It goes straight to the heart of WHY our neighborhoods, cities, infrastructure, schools, health, and people are perishing.

> **Isaiah 30:10**
>
> Which say to the seers, See not; and to the prophets, *prophesy* (H2372) not to us right things, speak to us smooth things, *prophesy* (H2372) deceits:

That is an assertive accusation against our seers and prophets, representing our scientific, political, and religious teachers today. No vision means telling us what we want to hear: smooth, flattering, positive things to make us feel good now. It doesn't matter if they are lies and deceit, just so long as it doesn't upset us! We want our leaders to give us the five-minute fix. Lose weight overnight, learn a language in a week, and overcome anxiety by being in the moment. We're treating major troubles with band-aids.

To put it plainly, mental health, which we're focusing on, is perishing, along with many other basics, like physical health, education, and well-being, etc., because we're not being taught what we ought.

The Contrast: Happy is He, and She

Again, he and she means all human beings, regardless of age, race, belief, nationality, and culture; all can be *happy* (H835). Does that mean full of laughs? No.

H835

אֶשֶׁר 'esher eh'-sher; from H833 (אָשַׁר); happiness; only in masculine plural construction as interjection, how happy!:

KJV - blessed, happy.

H833

אָשַׁר 'âshar aw-shar'; or אָשֵׁר; a primitive root; to be straight (used in the widest sense, especially to be level, right, happy); figuratively, to go forward, be honest, proper:

KJV - (call, be) bless(-ed, happy), go, guide, lead, relieve.

H838

אָשֻׁר 'âshur aw-shoor'; or אַשֻּׁר; from H833 (אָשַׁר) in the sense of going; a step:

KJV - going, step.

God designed humans to be happy and blessed. This state includes several concepts, which *The Explanation* will detail in this book. For now, grasp the overall picture. Again, the first point to note appears to be an incongruity *guide*: What has that got to do with happiness?

Proverbs 23:19

> Hear you, my son, and be wise, and *guide* (H833) your heart in the way.

Happy is he is the opposite of teachers with false vision. It is the teaching of a loving father to his son. It also involves guiding the heart, which represents the mind. The father teaches the proper way and encourages his son to follow that instruction, which leads to *blessings*. It involves going *forward* in the right direction, and H838 implies *step-by-step* progress.

Who Keeps the Law, Happy is He (and She)

After reading that sub-title, Is this what you're thinking? I know the word *law*, especially in an Old Testament context, has legalistic, sectarian, and fundamentalist connotations. But please allow me to explain because it is NOT that at all. Please don't take my word for it. Here are five verses from Proverbs that give you the contours of the hard-to-bear word *law*, as in "he that keeps the law, *happy* (H835) is he."

Proverbs 14:21

> He that despises his neighbour sins: but he that has mercy on the poor, *happy* (H835) is he.

Proverbs 16:20

> He that handles a matter wisely shall find good: and whoso trusts in the LORD, *happy* (H835) is he.

Proverbs 3:18

She [wisdom] is a tree of life to them that lay hold upon her: and *happy* (H833) is every one that retains her [wisdom].

Proverbs 9:6

Forsake the foolish, and live; and *go* (H833) in the way of *understanding* (H998).

Do you agree we should have mercy on the poor? Handle matters wisely? Trust in the Lord? Retain wisdom? Go in the way of understanding? Then, you agree wholeheartedly with the law.

Isaiah 1:17

Learn to do well seek judgment, *relieve* (H833) the oppressed, judge the fatherless, plead for the widow.

This law *relieves* the oppressed, those with anxiety and depression; this is the antidote, the way to natural relief. Part V of this book will elaborate on step-by-step ways to reach this relief.

This chapter opens our minds to one reason why God inspired the writing of an instruction manual: to give the steps to relieve mental illness, the most prevalent disease of the 21st Century. It reveals God's personal Interest and Involvement with everyone worldwide, regardless of who they are. Happy is he who comes upon God's Ways.

A Final Warning About Anxiety Coaches

I'm not saying that the myriad methods, some of which I'll cite later, are not helpful. They have light in them, which is why they draw convinced practitioners. I am saying that the result will be darkness simply because they do not point to God's Way. In fact, most lead in the opposite direction.

Isaiah 8:20

> To the *law* (the practical recommendations of God in Proverts) and to the testimony (in God's Word, the inspired Bible): if they speak not according to this word, it is because there is no light in them.

Be careful who your therapist is. Choose a Christian, Bible-oriented guide. With God's Help and Guidance, you can face anxiety and replace it with relief. Stay tuned; you can transform your mind and upgrade your life.

II. God Equipped Humans to Be Kings & Queens

God endowed all humans with the capacity to develop into Kings, Queens, and Priests.

Part II reveals HOW God equipped humans to accomplish His Plan for placing them on Earth.

9. Human Consciousness. The Breakthrough

Human consciousness and mind are among our turbulent age's most remarkable, if not the most significant, enigmas. Discover the facts.

It's all the more incredible because consciousness and mind are the basis of each human being.

In other words, we human beings, endowed with human consciousness, have no clue who or what we are! That must be the paradox to beat all paradoxes. We try to explain quantum physics and the universe; we can't even explain ourselves and why we can explain everything else!

We're starting Part II of *Mind Refreshed*, entitled, *How God Equipped Humans to be Kings and Queens,* and we'll discover the infinitely small and the astronomical gigantic.

Biblically, we can transform this statement into a question. In Chapter 1[1], we saw God created humans in His own image. So, how is God creating every human who has and will walk the surface of Earth in His image?

You can NOT upgrade your life correctly without adequately understanding the answer to those questions. It involves two components of each human: past, present, and future: human consciousness and mind, about which science, philosophy, and religion are in total darkness.

Human Consciousness and Human Darkness

Here are a few among hundreds of references to the absolute confusion reigning among scholars of human consciousness. This week, the renowned philosopher Daniel Dennett died. John Horgan, a science journalist and author I respect and have widely read, is known for his critical examinations of scientific theories and thinkers. He wrote in this article about the Dennett Paradox[2].

> When Dennett argues that we overrate consciousness, he demonstrates, paradoxically, how conscious he is, and he makes his audience more conscious. This "Dennett Paradox" is a rip-off,
>
> Of all the odd notions to emerge from debates over consciousness, the oddest is that it doesn't exist, at least not in the way we think it does. It is an illusion, like "Santa Claus" or "American democracy."
>
> Descartes said consciousness is the one undeniable fact of our existence, and I find it hard to disagree. I'm conscious

1. https://theexplanation.com/gods-creation-of-humans-why-divine-purpose/

2. https://johnhorgan.org/cross-check/consciousness-and-the-dennett-paradox

> right now, as I type this sentence, and you are presumably conscious as you read it...
>
> The idea that consciousness isn't real has always struck me as crazy, but smart people espouse it. One of the smartest is philosopher Daniel Dennett, who has been questioning consciousness for decades, notably in his 1991 bestseller *Consciousness Explained.*

Note that Descartes's consciousness is the one undeniable fact of our existence. *The Explanation* agrees wholeheartedly and will prove it Biblically. Human consciousness and mind are inseparable, as I'll show you. It is impossible to correctly transform your mind without adequately understanding these elementary components of all humans.

Supposing you're interested in pursuing in-depth knowledge about the confusion that reigns in understanding consciousness and mind. In that case, I highly recommend Robert Khun, whom I know personally, and his interviews with world-renowned scientists, philosophers, and religionists on his website Closer to Truth[3]. One debated subject is: Does Human Consciousness have a Special Purpose? I will answer that below, but you will quickly realize that his scholarly guests wax eloquent but come up empty-handed regarding specifics about human consciousness.

Ignorance of Human Consciousness

To top off this section, here are a few quotes, among many, that reveal our incomprehension about this subject.

1. **Daniel Dennett**: "There is no such thing as consciousness and no such thing as free will. (...) Free will is a myth, and so is consciousness, pure introspectable conscious experience."

3. https://closertotruth.com/search-results/?searchwp=consciousness

2. **Patricia Churchland**: "There is no magical moment when consciousness suddenly appears in a brain. That would be to adopt a dualistic view that sees consciousness as separate from the brain."
3. **Paul Churchland**: "The thought of there being such a thing as 'consciousness'... over and above the physical goings-on in the body is a notion fraught with conceptual peril."
4. **David Chalmers**: (though he's known for his work on the *hard problem* of consciousness, he's been interpreted as expressing doubt): "Despite widespread agreement that consciousness arises from a physical basis, there is little consensus on the nature of that basis."
5. **Susan Blackmore**: "Consciousness is not some mysterious 'other stuff' that needs its own special science because it does not exist."

It's important to note that the idea that consciousness does not exist is not a mainstream position among scientists. Still, some philosophers and scientists have proposed skeptical views on consciousness, and some may advocate for different interpretations of consciousness rather than outright denial of its existence.

Philosophy, religion, and science are at odds regarding this fundamental subject. The result of this confusion is mental illness because we don't know how to prevent it or how to cure it. How can you fix anything when you don't know what it is, nor why it exists?

Why We Need Human Consciousness

If you need a printing press to render four colors, you must equip it with the necessary components, such as tubes to feed the different colors, rollers to transfer them, etc. A satisfactory result is impossible if we don't furnish all the parts.

Why did God create humankind, and what result does God want for each human? That's Part I: ultimately, to be Kings, Queens, and Priests. To reach that goal, each human must realize they have a depraved mind and make a free will decision to transform their mind to socialization and rulership ethics that lead to peace with their Creator and their fellow humans. If humans were made out of wood or steel, could they do this? No.

If the human body were equipped with Artificial Intelligence, could it recognize that it needs a behavioral change? No. At its core, AI operates within the framework of binary code, with complex algorithms and neural networks being represented and manipulated through sequences of binary digits (0's and 1's). This relationship underscores the computational nature of AI, as it relies on the precise manipulation of binary data to perform tasks.

Scholars recognize that consciousness is not solely a product of computational processes; it lacks the subjective experience and self-awareness characteristic of consciousness. The nature of consciousness remains poorly understood, with scientists grappling to define its fundamental properties and mechanisms. Without a clear understanding of what consciousness entails, it is impossible for inorganic material to be endowed with human consciousness; this is the heart of the *hard problem* referred to by David Chalmers above.

Consciousness and mind, coupled together, are the only components that allow humans to accomplish God's Plan: be aware of and acknowledge their sinfulness, recognize their misbehavior, which leads to mental illness and anxiety, come out of Babylon, and make a concerted decision to step onto the path that leads to spiritual Jerusalem and peace of mind.

Neshama, the Cornerstone of Being Human

That's why Genesis 2:7 is fundamentally the most crucial verse for understanding what it is to be human.

> **Genesis 2:7**
>
> And the LORD God formed man of the dust of the ground, and breathed into his nostrils the *breath* of life; and man became a living soul.

Breath in, "breath of life," reveals the key to grasping what a human is and the components God breathed into him and endowed him with to accomplish the tasks God set before each one of us.

Breath is *neshama* in Biblical Hebrew; only a deep understanding of what it is and how it functions yields the God-given way to transform your mind and upgrade your life. Part II reveals how God equipped each human with the exact and perfect spiritual mechanism to resolve anxiety, face adversity, support hardship, and come out victorious. It also explains how God is and will accomplish His goals through reticent, even rebellious humans and how He has endowed us with excellent qualities to move forward when we walk in step with Him.

10. Paranormal Activity: Real or Not?

Does paranormal activity like levitation, after-death experiences, ghosts, multiple personalities, voices, flying objects, haunted houses, and possessed persons exist? Is there conclusive evidence? Yes.

And more: Automatic writing, painting, singing, speaking, and other paranormal activities. What to make of them? Are they scams or real? Does the immaterial spirit world exist? Why ask such questions?

If such phenomena are a reality, they defy the scientific method, which depends on empirical, observable, verifiable, and testable evidence with measured results. To be clear, energy and the minutest elemental particles that travel in waves, although invisible, are still material, composed of atoms, protons, neutrons, and the smallest quarks. Science has made incredible progress in discovering the Universe's building blocks. That's the material reality. But science denies paranormal activity and, at the very least, shuns anything non-material.

The ultimate question related to whether paranormal activity is real is the clash between monism and dualism. Does everything have only a physical, material origin (monism), or additionally, are there immaterial, intangible, supernatural essences (dualism)?

In this book, *Mind Refreshed*, the author discusses whether mind and consciousness are derivatives and, therefore, part of the brain (monism, science's perspective) or outside of the brain, belonging to the supernatural realm (dualism). If we give evidence for paranormal activity, then dualism must be considered a natural phenomenon.

Examples of Paranormal and Supernatural Cannot be Denied

There is so much evidence of paranormal activity that major websites and stores have dedicated libraries of books[1] to these mysterious, dreadful, but true encounters[2].

The Explanation has written extensively about sound people who have personally experienced supernatural effects. Please watch this video about paranormal activity and its genuine influence on individuals[3]; it's a chapter from the book *Mind-Body Problem Solved*. Also, read this article about Mind Control[4] from the book *Agony of Humankind and the Antidote*.

1. https://www.goodreads.com/shelf/show/paranormal-library
2. https://www.dailymail.co.uk/sciencetech/article-12291233/Paranormal-experiences-common-encounters-experts-think-mean.html
3. https://youtu.be/defup0zmO7I
4. https://theexplanation.com/mind-control-the-serpents-number-one-goal/

This TED Talk by Elizabeth Gilbert[5], a best-selling author, on *Your Elusive Creative Genious* is enlightening, and I encourage you to watch it. She shares the radical idea that, instead of the rare person *being* a genius, all of us *have* a genius. You cannot escape this lucid explanation without understanding that something non-material exists. If you don't want to call it divine or spiritual, that's fine; refer to it as metaphysical—without physical presence or abstract.

Paranormal Activity Exists, Dualism Reigns

The logical conclusion *The Explanation* draws from paranormal activity is that its existence is reality.

WARNING: Avoid such harmful occupations. It is serious, and its practice can cause damaging results. We must talk about it and will return to this subject. We acknowledge the existence of paranormal activity but disapprove of its practice for our own sanity.

The only reason *The Explanation* proves its evidence is to demonstrate, without a doubt, a non-physical world outside of our material world. This second invisible, ethereal, immaterial realm exists and is as authentic as our tangible physical environment.

In other words, dualism and not monism is the correct state of the Universe.

The Nature of Neshama

Now, let's apply this understanding to the subject at hand, the nature of human beings. Let's expand Genesis 2:7.

Genesis 2:7

5. https://www.ted.com/talks/elizabeth_gilbert_your_elusive_creative_genius

> And the Lord God formed man of the dust of the ground, and breathed into his nostrils the *breath* (H5397) of life, and man became a living soul.

The word *breath* appears twice in English in this verse. In Biblical Hebrew, they are two totally different words, each with its significant meaning. For now, we'll focus only on *breath* in *breath of life*. When we read this in our native language, we think of the air we breathe, which is correct; it is a physical element insofar as science is concerned. Unfortunately, the translation only renders a partial understanding of this word.

> **H5397** (check it at UnlockBibleMeaning.com[6])
>
> נְשָׁמָה nᵉshâmâh nesh-aw-maw'; from H5395 (נָשַׁם); a puff, i.e. wind, angry or vital breath, divine inspiration, intellect. or (concretely) an animal:
>
> KJV - blast, (that) breath(-eth), inspiration, soul, spirit.

The 17th-century King James translators used five English words to render this one Biblical Hebrew word. Note that two of them, *inspiration* and *spirit*, are immaterial. We will return to *soul* later. This primary verse about the Creation of the first human being plunges us into dualism. On one side, we have a body of dust, including the brain and the air we breathe.

On the other hand, we have neshama, which represents the paranormal activity of *inspiration* and *spirit*. In this context, I'm using *paranormal* simply with its Greek grammatical meaning of *para* as a prefix: besides: alongside: beyond: aside from. In other words, it is separate from the *normal* material realm.

6. https://UnlockBibleMeaning.com

I remind you we have already given definitive evidence for the reality of paranormal activity. We should not be surprised to find its base at Creation in the most profound verse about the origin of humankind.

This quote from Dr. Robert Epstein[7] (PhD in Experimental Psychology and former editor of Psychology Today[8]) was never so valid.

> A successful understanding of the mind–brain relationship will necessarily involve understanding the brain as a transduction device in one way or another. Such an understanding could prove enormously fruitful and can help us move beyond the current materialist framework in which neuroscience is practiced, which has held us so far back in our understanding of the mind and the brain. The brain is obviously material but it is just as obvious that the mind has immaterial abilities.

Dr. Epstein refers to the mind as having immaterial abilities. That's correct, but it omits consciousness, also an immaterial paranormal activity.

Neshama Endows Humans with Inspiration, which is Consciousness

This unique spiritual element was thrust into humans by their Creator God. We will focus on it and its accompanying spirit, ruach, which we'll see in an upcoming chapter because together, they make humans human. Each person uses them to make themselves into what they become. Hence, neshama and ruach are the basis of *Mind Refreshed*. That's why we must spend time establishing the solution to the

7. https://en.wikipedia.org/wiki/Robert_Epstein

8. https://www.psychologytoday.com

Mind-Body Problem. Without this base, we cannot develop the God-intended Biblical way to avoid and heal anxiety for everyone in the 21st century.

Similarly, from God's Biblical Point of View, by infusing humans with neshama and ruach, God shows us HOW He equipped us with the essential and necessary capacities to develop into Kings, Queens, and Priests[9].

What Neshama Confers on Human Beings

The Explanation simply answers what the qualities of neshama are by referring to God's Word.

> **Job 32:8**
>
> But there is a spirit in man: and the *inspiration* (H5397 - neshama) of the Almighty gives them *understanding* (H995).

Neshama confers *understanding* on you, me, and every human who has or will walk the face of Earth. Let the Bible define *understanding*.

> **H995**
>
> בִּין bîyn bene; a primitive root; to separate mentally (or distinguish), i.e.(generally) understand:
>
> KJV - attend, consider, be cunning, diligently, direct, **discern**, eloquent, feel, inform, instruct, have intelligence, know, look well to, **mark**, **perceive**, be prudent, regard, (can) skill(-full), teach, think, (cause, make to, get, give, have) understand(-ing), view, (deal) wise(-ly, man).

9. https://theexplanation.com/gods-creation-of-earth-why-decoding-divine-plan/

The KJV translations of H995 are non-material qualities each human possesses, obviously at different levels, but they characterize humans. I highly recommend you expand your understanding of neshama by watching Breath of Life. The Unique Possessors of Neshama on Earth[10] and Neshama is Translated Inspiration. Discover Deeper Meaning[11]

We have established the existence of paranormal activity to show evidence for dualism, the physical and spiritual worlds. Genesis 2:7 clearly reveals the biblical fact that God breathed neshama into the first human's body of dust, establishing this dualism (Genesis 2:7). This neshama is God's *Inspiration*[12] (Job 32:8), endowing humans with *understanding*, a *mark of discernment or perception. The Explanation* transposes this meaning into modern terminology: *consciousness.*

Together, the neshama and ruach are the elements we work with in humans to transform our minds and upgrade our lives. We're getting the basis of human psychology right.

10. https://youtu.be/jtREpyH1deU

11. https://youtu.be/PCyduivIGwM

12. https://theexplanation.com/neshama-inspiration-discover-the-deeper-meaning/

11. Evolution Debunked: Humans' Neshama

Only Humans, not animals, are endowed with neshama, direct from God. Humans are a unique species related explicitly to their Creator. Biblical proof unveiled.

God's Plan (His WHY Create the Universe and humanity?) involves transforming every free-willed human into Kings, Queens, and Priests. God had to equip humans to accomplish this program. HOW does He achieve this feat? By giving each human the immaterial neshama and ruach. In the last chapter, we saw God breathed the *breath* (H5397) of life into the first human. In Biblical Hebrew, that's neshama.

God and Only Humans On Earth Possess Neshama

Neshama isn't just any breath; it's unique. The Bible affirms that God alone gives neshama, inhabiting every human being—but humans alone, as we shall see.

Job 33:4

> The Spirit of God has made me, and the *breath* (H5397) of the Almighty has given me life.

The Almighty has given only humans some of His own Neshama, His possession. Remember, we discussed humans being Godkind[1]. God created humans in His image. He did so by placing a portion of Himself in each of us through the neshama of life, the breath of life. I use a small "n" because we possess a minute human portion. Our destiny is to inherit Neshama with a capital "N," and that's when God will transform us into Kings, Queens, and Priests.

Job 27:3

> All the while my *breath* (says Job, H5397) is in me, and the spirit of God is in my nostrils;

Job was a wise man with a spiritual understanding of *neshama*. He knew he possessed it, unlike most people today. He also knew that the *spirit* of God animated him; the prophet Isaiah confirms this fundamental psychological knowledge of what a human being is.

Isaiah 42:5

> Thus says God the LORD, he that created the heavens, and stretched them out; he that spread forth the earth, and that which comes out of it; he that gives *breath* (H5397) to the people upon it, and spirit to them that walk therein:

1. https://theexplanation.com/gods-creation-of-humans-why-divine-purpose/

Another context revealing God gives neshama AND spirit to ALL people on Earth. He is an inclusive God. All people are His Creation, and He has a purpose for each of us. We are living a given instant in that Creation Plan, but there's much more to come.

Job 32:8

> But there is a spirit in man: and the *inspiration* (H5397) of the Almighty gives them understanding.

Both the Almighty and humans possess neshama, and this verse states that neshama, an immaterial essence, confers specific attributes associated with *understanding* on humans, precisely what we'll learn in the following chapters.

Can you see how the English word *breath* is far short of expressing what neshama really is? The Job 32:8 translation *inspiration* is closer. As it says in that same verse *of the Almighty*, I think a better translation of neshama would be *Divine Essence* (the Almighty's Breath).

Psalm 150:6

> Let every thing that has *breath* (H5397) praise the LORD. Praise you the Lord.

This verse is the last in the final Psalm; it concludes the entire book. To highlight its importance, this is the only occurrence of *neshama* related to humans in the entire 150 Psalms. It ends God's Plan for humanity and opens up a new era, revealing a state of peace, prosperity, and unity between all beings with their Creator, Savior, and God. All in that position will possess well-oriented neshama and, as a result, will know God and be able to praise Him. Instead of *breath,* translate it *Divine Essence*. Isn't it clearer?

Only Humans Possess Neshama, NOT Animals

Now, it's time to debunk evolution. Above, we see that God shared His Neshama with humans. On no occasion does the Bible say animals possess this Divine Essence. In fact, God's Word reveals that animals do NOT possess neshama.

> **Joshua 10:40, 11:11,14**
>
> 10:40 So Joshua (on entering the Promised Land) smote all the country of the hills, and of the south, and of the vale, and of the springs, and all their kings: he left none remaining, but utterly destroyed all that *breathed* (H5397 - neshama), as the LORD God of Israel commanded.
>
> 11:11 And they smote all the souls that were therein with the edge of the sword, utterly destroying them: there was not any left to breathe (H5397 neshama): and he burnt Hazor with fire.
>
> 14 And all the spoil of these cities, and the cattle, the children of Israel took for a prey to themselves; but every man they smote with the edge of the sword, until they had destroyed them, neither left they any to *breathe* (H5397).

In this episode, as the children of Israel entered the Promised Land, they utterly destroyed all the souls (Jos. 11:11) with neshama (*breathe*, as it's translated here). But they took the cattle for prey. If they destroyed ALL those with neshama and kept the cattle alive, then, by deduction, cattle do NOT have neshama.

Furthermore, cattle BREATHE. Therefore, we cannot limit the meaning of neshama to *breathing*. There is something humans possess, given by Yahveh, breathed into them that animals do not have. It is neshama, and it behooves us to know what this is. Neshama differentiates humans from animals.

This understanding is also the solution to the *hard problem* of consciousness, which is how the mind evolved from the lesser, almost non-existent animal state to the far superior human state. Well, it didn't evolve at all; God gives only humans neshama.

ANIMALS DO NOT POSSESS NESHAMA. This vital knowledge totally differentiates humans from animals and explains the impassible chasm separating them. Do you realize the impact of this Bible comprehension on philosophy, religion, and sciences like social behavior, which studies animals to understand why humans act the way we do? Do you see that saying chimps and humans share 98.8% of their physical DNA[2] completely omits the fact that chimps do not possess neshama, but only humans do? Do you see why we first have to establish what consciousness and mind are before we can have our *Mind Refreshed?*

Please read the story of Nebuchadnezzar (Daniel Chapter 4 in *Mind-Body Problem Solved*[3], or watch the video[4]), who lost his understanding for seven years and was transformed into an animal. Afterward, he regained his wisdom, recuperated his Kingship, and recognized the one true God. God performed these miraculous transformations of Nebuchadnezzar's mind; He removed Nebuchadnezzar's neshama and reinstalled it seven years later. Without neshama, one is NOT human.

Watch[5] or read[6] Chapter 22 of the book *Mind-Body Problem Solved* because a controversial verse in Genesis 7:22 seems to indicate animals

2. https://www.amnh.org/exhibitions/permanent/human-origins/understanding-our-past/dna-comparing-humans-and-chimps

3. *https://theexplanation.com/neshama-inspiration-discover-the-deeper-meaning/*

4. https://youtu.be/PCyduivIGwM

DO possess neshama. You must understand the correct meaning of this verse. Animals do not possess this unique spirit.

More Evidence: Only Humans Possess Neshama

We'll end this chapter by comparing how Strong erroneously defined H995 *understanding* and H5397 *intellect.*

> **H995**
>
> בִּין bîyn bene; a primitive root; to separate mentally (or distinguish), i.e. (generally) understand:

Now, look at Strong's definition of neshama. See if you can catch it.

> **H5397**
>
> נְשָׁמָה n^{e}shâmâh nesh-aw-maw'; from H5395 (נָשַׁם); a puff, i.e. wind, angry or vital breath, divine inspiration, intellect. or (concretely) an animal:

The error is *(concretely) an animal.* James Strong confused humans with animals. Darwin published *On the Origin of Species* in 1859 and *The Descent of Man and Selection in Relation to Sex* in 1871. Strong finished his Concordance in 1890, so it's possible this supposed scientific knowledge influenced him. Together with the unheard-of understanding of neshama, I'm amazed at how little, not to say nothing, exists about this vital entity even today. Theology is silent.

To drive home Strong's H955 reference to *separate mentally (or distinguish)* only humans from all other life forms, notice that H996, the following Biblical Hebrew word after H995 (*understanding* in Job

---

5. https://youtu.be/Y2dMzKMoThw

6. https://theexplanation.com/neshamah-and-ruach-ultimate-backbone-of-humans/

32:8), is identical in Hebrew; compare the Hebrew letters. H996 means *between*, or a *space between*, as you can see in Genesis 1:4, concerning the opposition between darkness and light. Neshama distinguishes only humans and puts light years *between* them and all other living creatures.

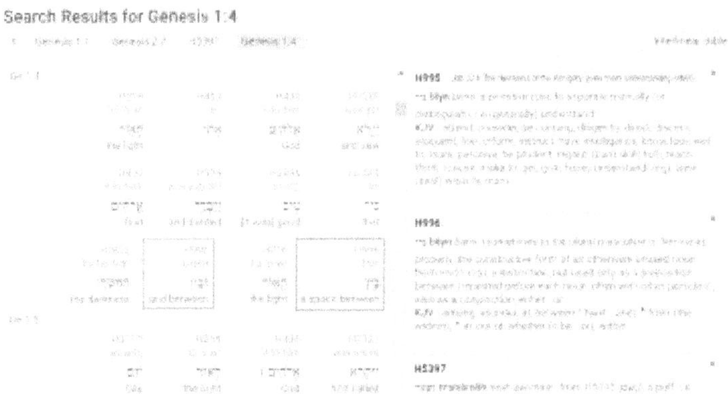

Figure 1. Genesis 1:4 in the Interlinear Bible

We have now established HOW God equipped only humans to function with neshama: consciousness, awareness, and understanding. That's where mental health begins. We must let God's Word reveal HOW consciousness and mind, neshama and ruach, two immaterial spirits, work together. That is the basis for knowing WHAT practical steps we must take to nurture and heal the human mental capacity.

We cannot apply evolutionary behavioral therapy with dreams of complete success when humans are not the result of evolution. Humans are a unique species, the ONLY one with God's Neshama. We will move on to the practical aspect of how to nurture and heal only when we understand this base.

We have now established HOW God equipped only humans to function with neshama: consciousness, awareness, and understanding. That's where mental health begins.

12. Reasoning, the Primary Human Quality

Humans possess Reasoning because God endowed us with His Neshama. We are in His Image, He reasons. Likewise, we possess this quality—the inside scoop into this unique human trait.

Humans are set apart as unique living beings on Earth because they are the sole proprietors (Joshua 11:14) of the God-given spirit *neshama* (Genesis 2:7 *breath* of life), which confers on each human Godly *understanding* (Job 38:2), also translated *perception* and *discernment* (H995); this is the basis of human mentality, which we call consciousness and awareness.

God transferred a human portion of His Divine Consciousness to humans, making each one of us *in His image.*

The first chapters of the Bible, Genesis, reveal the five fundamental qualities of being human that set us light-years apart from animals and put us on the God plane. They are reasoning, purpose, conduct, socialization, and rulership. Over the following few chapters, I'll elaborate on each of them. This chapter is devoted to Reasoning.

Figure 2. Five aspects of consciousness

Humans are unique; we have a mode of reasoning and behavioral functioning that soar above all other creatures on Earth. Why? Because humans are Godkind, He reasons and functions very sophisticatedly and imparts those same faculties to us.

At Creation, God breathed a human portion of His own Neshama, the *neshama (breath) of life*, into the first human, Adam (Job 33:4 verify it at UnlockBibleMeaning.com[1]). Neshama confers understanding on all humans (Job 32:8); this is synonymous with awareness or consciousness. Our consciousness is characterized by five main qualities, like God's.

This chapter considers *reasoning*: "For my thoughts are not your thoughts, neither are your ways my ways, says the LORD" (Isaiah 55:8). This establishes that God and humans think and reason, although not on the same level.

Reasoning – the First Trait of Consciousness

1. https://unlockbiblemeaning.com/

In the Bible, we have one of the clearest examples of reasoning with Eve. First, God gave her facts; then, the Serpent fed her fake facts. Finally, she reasoned and made a fatally wrong decision based on intuition. Via His Neshama, God transmitted this capability of reasoning to each human.

Human understanding grapples with five key realms of inquiry, each trying to illuminate the intricacies of existence and human nature. As individuals we tend toward one or the other. The first four are human reasoning; the fifth is God's.

1. Observation, Intuition

Humanity's primary mode of gathering information lays the foundation for reasoning. Reliable facts stem from accurate observation, yet interpreting these observations must also be trustworthy. Just as fake news distorts reality, flawed interpretations can lead to misconceptions. Hence, both the source and interpretation of observations and intuition are crucial for establishing genuine understanding.

Likewise, gut feelings and personal conclusions can be misleading. Can wisdom and truth come from dual-natured human beings? This deceptive idea is *listening to your heart* or your *inner voice*. Can inward searching into flawed hearts and minds yield faithful and valid discernment?

2. Philosophy

Philosophy, the pursuit of wisdom, delves into the fundamental questions of existence and the universe's interconnectedness. It seeks to unravel the mysteries of life, pondering the meaning of human existence and the purpose behind our presence in the cosmos. From spiritual enlightenment to metaphysical inquiries, philosophy traverses diverse avenues of thought, offering insights into the nature of reality and human consciousness.

3. Science

Science, regarded as the savior of our world, embodies human reasoning and inquiry, aiming to decipher the mysteries of the universe through empirical observation and logical deduction. From quantum mechanics to sensory perception, science unveils the workings of the natural world and advances technological innovations that address global challenges. Despite its limitations, science remains a cornerstone of modern civilization, driving progress, shaping human understanding of reality, and even delving into human conduct.

4. Religion

Despite the rise of science, religion continues to wield considerable influence over human reasoning, with billions of individuals adhering to diverse belief systems worldwide. Whether monotheistic or polytheistic, religion offers frameworks for understanding the metaphysical realm and provides moral guidance for adherents. From religious experiences to doctrinal interpretations, faith shapes human perspectives and motivates ethical conduct across cultures and civilizations.

5. Theology

Often overlooked yet integral to understanding, theology is not just the human study of God. It is the profound search for the God-intended meaning of life. It's finding where He

> scripted His intentions and what He has in mind for His Creation. What does God have to say? Where are His Scriptures? What is His reasoning?

Human-concocted religious beliefs and traditions are not our basis. Theology explores the Divine Intent in the sacred Word of God and seeks to elucidate the reasoning of the Higher Power. We try to discern this Godly Wisdom and guidance from a superior being to puny humans. Such believers shape their worldview and moral convictions on His Doings and Sayings, convinced that He knows best what human conduct needs; this is the way to beat anxiety.

These five realms of reasoning illuminate different facets of existence and offer diverse perspectives on the mysteries of life. Each realm contributes to humanity's collective pursuit of wisdom and enlightenment, but only the latter gives insights into Godly Wisdom.

Consciousness is the closest issue to being human; the first four methods of reasoning are empty-headed without accurate explanations. Theology alone, as demonstrated in this volume and *Mind-Body Problem Solved*, reveals the origin and essence of consciousness. Haste the day when this is common knowledge; these sure fundamentals will be the foundation of reasoning and human conduct.

Addendum: Learning is progressive; we don't get it in one fell swoop. When I started the Biblical Hebrew study of Genesis around 2008, I had no idea about the meaning of *breath of life*—neshama. A 500-page book about *Mind-Body Problem Solved* was not even an idea. The concept of the five Biblical aspects of consciousness arose as I wrote that book, and I used the triangular Maslow approach[2] to present them. Later in the book, I explained why I switched to a circular

2. https://theexplanation.com/astonishing-meaning-what-it-means-to-be-human/

presentation[3]. Now, in *Mind Refreshed,* I've made a further update, placing Reasoning at the head of the five aspects.

Reasoning is at the origin of Purpose, Conduct, Socialization, and Rulership. God gave us neshama and ruach, so we think and reason like He does.

The first deviation from God is by Lucifer, who twisted his reasoning process, "For you have said in your heart, I will ascend into heaven" (Isaiah 14:13). *Said in your heart* is a Bible expression for reasoning. And the Serpent continues to twist people's minds. God allows people to be blinded and follow their *imaginations* (G1261 reasoning, thought) (Romans 1:21). Reasoning is where it all starts; that is what we must refresh.

Romans 12:2 "...be you transformed by the renewing of your *mind,* (G3563 Strong: in thought feeling or will) that you may prove what is that good, and acceptable, and perfect, will of God." This verse is the reason the working title was "Transform Your Mind Upgrade Your Life." **Mind *Refreshed*** represents this transformation from our way to God's Way of Reasoning.

I'm explaining this here because when you read previous books and the links from this book to previous blog posts, the information about reasoning will be correct. However, the order of the five aspects of consciousness does not reflect this updated version: Reasoning, Purpose, Conduct, Socialization, and Rulership.

3. https://theexplanation.com/psychology-best-bible-definition-for-humans/

13. Purpose Unveiled: A Human Trait

The mystery of *purpose* and human *conduct* are the second and third traits conferred on humans by God's Neshama, making us in His image.

We'll also see seven qualities of *human conduct* typified by Christ's Ministry, God on Earth. The next chapter includes the two remaining qualities of *socialization* and *rulership*.

God Has Purpose

Here's how we know God's Neshama possesses the trait of Purpose.

> **Genesis 2:7**
>
> And the LORD God *formed* (H3335) man of the dust of the ground, and breathed into his nostrils the breath of life; and man became a living soul.

Let's see the Biblical Hebrew meaning.

> **H3335**
>
> יָצַר yâtsar yaw-tsar'; probably identical with H3334 (יָצַר) (through the squeezing into shape); (compare H3331 (יָצַע)); to mould into a form; especially as a potter; figuratively, to determine (i.e. form a resolution):
>
> KJV – × earthen, fashion, form, frame, make(-r), potter, purpose.

Whether it's Strong's definition, *squeeze into shape, form a resolution*, or the KJV translator's exact translation *purpose*, it's clear that when God formed the first human, He had a long-term project in mind—just like a potter who, when they put the clay on the wheel, has in their mind a picture of the final product.

Here's God's Challenge to atheists and doubters:

> **Isaiah 29:16**
>
> Shall the work [humans] say of him [God] that made it, He made me not? Or shall the thing *framed* (H3336) say of him that *framed* (H3335) it, He had no *understanding* (H995)?

Humans call into question God's Consciousness and Understanding; we'd be better off at least paying a little attention to His Word, where God says He has a purpose for creating us.

Humans Alone Possess Purpose

Do humans have the quality of *yatsar*, purpose? At UnlockBibleMeaning.com[1], in Strong's Concordance with the H3335

1. https://unlockbiblemeaning.com/

reference displayed on the right, click on *Hebrew Concordance for H3335*. Here are a couple of verses confirming that we have the same image of God in that we inherently possess purpose.

Psalm 94:20

Shall the throne of iniquity have fellowship with you [humans], which *frames* (H3335) mischief by a law?

Isaiah 44:12

The smith with the tongs both works in the coals, and *fashions* (H3335) it with hammers, and works it with the strength of his arms...

Only God and humans are purpose-driven, yatsar beings. That's because we're in His Image.

Aspects of Purpose

We can subdivide this human singularity into many more qualities that endow every human being. Click the links for a more profound view of these human characteristics.

1. **Space-Time** is Not Only a Scientific Theory, but It's Also a Human Singularity[2] (1.2 in the book *Audit of Humankind*)

Each of us has 24 hours (our time) to manage whatever we want (our space). It consists of 8 hours (time) of work in a space like a home, office, factory, truck, or ship—eight hours in your bedroom, sleeping, and recreation time in a

2. https://theexplanation.com/space-time-is-not-only-scientific-theory-its-also-a-human-singularity/

space like a forest. Your space includes every physical item you use, including the intangibles like the air you breathe, the electricity to run the tools, the kitchen's odors, or the gymnasium's heat. Humans alone manage their space-time.

2. **Creativity** Sets Humankind Apart from and Above All Other Life on Earth[3] (1.3)

I'm amazed by the inventiveness of human ingenuity, aren't you? There are myriad ways to cook food, decorate a room, build a house, catch fish, turn wood, etc. God is the Creator, and the neshama equips every human with the ability to invent objects, ideas, and ways of accomplishing tasks. It's never-ending.

3. **Imagination**—Another Singularity of Humankind in Your Consciousness[4] (1.4)

Whenever a writer throws words on a page, an artist dips their brush in paint, or a designer sketches lines on a serviette in a restaurant, they imagine. We've filled our consumer society with merchandise that started in someone's conceptualizing mind. Each product was first a figment of a creator's imagination, a flash of insight, a daydream, or maybe even a nightdream. Imagination is where everything starts. That's why Reasoning is the foremost aspect of consciousness, as we saw in the last chapter. Humans imagine because they possess consciousness, neshama.

---

3. https://theexplanation.com/creativity-sets-humankind-apart-from-and-above-all-other-life-on-earth/

4. https://theexplanation.com/imagination-another-singularity-of-humankind-in-your-mind/

4. Bears Don't **Learn** to Ride Bicycles. Humans Learn That and Much More[5] (1.5)

To learn is a lifelong endeavor. It starts with how to suck your mother's nipple and ends with how to get out of bed with an arthritis-wracked body. There always was, is, and will be something new to understand. When humans look up at the cloudy sky and wonder about the weather, pick up their daily newspaper, listen to the news, or watch it on their mobile phones, they learn about the world around them and themselves. When consciousness stops, learning stops.

5. Your **Choices** Tell Us Who You Are. In Fact, They Identify You[6] (1.6)

Every human being has a choice over various aspects of their life. Humankind is one race, but through choice, we're 8 billion individuals. Through our consciousness, we choose our hairdo, what we read or watch, the causes we support, and the ideas we propagate.

6. **Growth** Mindset—A Frame of Mind Unique to Humankind[7] (1.7)

Consciousness confers on humans the thrill of making progress and seeing oneself and others improve their lives. Not just earning more money or living in a luxury house. But progress is like piling blocks one on top of each other, learning the alphabet, riding a bicycle, mastering the waltz,

5. https://theexplanation.com/bears-dont-learn-to-ride-bicycles-humans-learn-that-and-much-more/
6. https://theexplanation.com/your-choices-tell-us-who-you-are-in-fact-they-identify-you/
7. https://theexplanation.com/growth-mindset-unique-humankind/

and driving a car. So, daily, we make incremental improvements to our life experiences.

> 7. I **Challenge** you… A Human Trait that Keeps Us Moving Forward[8] (1.8)
>
> Whether it's a face-off over a game of Monopoly or a personal test to obtain one's driver's license, the challenge is a uniquely human characteristic. Over two billion people step up to the challenge of playing video games. That's about one in four people worldwide. Huge. Why do they play? It's fun, but it's also a challenge. We're trying to beat something. Better our score, faster, more accurate, and more skillful. We all have personal records that we're proud of, but we always try to improve; this is an aspect of consciousness necessary for the purpose of life.

Edifying, nurturing young minds, and healing depressed, anxious minds means guiding people to see why they're here now. It encourages them to find and activate their innate creativity, imagination, learning, growth, and personal challenge to focus on their big purpose in life.

Having a Purpose is Primary in Life's Trajectory

Neither Science nor Psychology understands the origin of this uniquely human trait, yet they grasp the importance of having a plan with objectives.

> He who has a why to live for can bear almost any how.
>
> — Friedrich Nietzsche.

---

8. https://theexplanation.com/challenge-accompanied-courage-needed-face-new-struggles-another-human-singularity/

The purpose of life is not to be happy. It is to be useful, to be honorable, to be compassionate, to have it make some difference that you have lived and lived well.

— Ralph Waldo Emerson

Nothing is more creative… nor destructive… than a brilliant mind with a purpose.

— Dan Brown, Inferno

Make your work to be in keeping with your purpose.

— Leonardo da Vinci

You can have anything you want if you want it badly enough. You can be anything you want to be, do anything you set out to accomplish if you hold to that desire with singleness of purpose.

— Abraham Lincoln

What's Your Purpose?

Although science and psychology are ignorant of the origin of establishing and striving toward a long-term mission, they fully know its importance on the human psyche. This book, *Mind Refreshed*, is based on God's Word. However, the principles elaborated on are valid for all humans regardless of their individual characteristics. No matter your present situation, prince or pauper, happy or unhappy, sick or healthy, employed or jobless, the main point to grasp to uplift your life is to aim for an objective.

Life is an arrow heading for its target; you must plunge toward your aspiration. You must establish your mission in life. Your goal is to find your purpose. There are many excellent free and paid resources in libraries and on the internet. Here's an article with fifteen key questions[9] to get you started.

If you're lost, just focus and meditate on your long-term purpose in life. It will come, and as you journey, you'll find all sorts of challenges that necessitate imaginative solutions that will put you on or maintain a path to improved mental health.

Human Conduct – the Third Trait of Consciousness

The essence of human conduct can be encapsulated in seven key points, each reflecting a facet of our complex nature and interactions with each other and the world. These are the primary characteristics of how each of us functions. We possess all of them from one degree to another, and their application or not is one cause of our anxiety. Read the details in *Audit of Humankind*[10].

1. Two-faced Humanity

Humanity's complexity lies in its dual nature, where individuals exhibit both virtue and vice. This dichotomy, present in everyone from priests to criminals, underscores the unique moral agency inherent to humanity. The consequences of this dual behavior can range from admirable deeds to catastrophic comportment, highlighting the profound impact of human actions on ourselves, our fellow humans, and the world around us.

2. Free Will

---

9. https://www.bravethinkinginstitute.com/blog/life-transformation/ask-these-15-questions-to-help-you-discover-your-life-purpose

10. *https://theexplanation.com/read-all-the-content-of-audit-of-humankind-online/*

At the core of human existence lies the capacity for free will, granting individuals the power to make choices and shape their destinies; you chose to read this chapter. However, exercising free will is not always straightforward and is often constrained by external circumstances. Despite these limitations, each person navigates myriad choices, from the mundane to the profound, ultimately charting their own course of conduct through life.

3. **Human Behavior** as an Expression of Two-Faced Humans and Free Will

Human behavior emerges from the interplay of dual-faced and free will, forming a unique amalgamation of individual traits and choices. This behavioral landscape, shaped by factors such as heredity, environment, and social education or lack thereof, coupled with free will decisions, reflects how each individual paints their life portrait by deciding the shades of good and evil they'll apply to their canvas.

4. **Ethics** as the Blueprint for Behavior

Ethics are the guiding principles that govern human behavior, providing a moral compass for navigating life's complexities. From the rules of sportsmanship to the laws of the land, ethical standards permeate every aspect of society, ensuring order and harmony. Without these foundational principles, society would become chaotic, lacking the cohesion necessary for peaceful coexistence.

5. **Justice** and its Relationship with Ethics

Justice enforces ethical norms, ensuring adherence to societal standards through rewards and penalties. By upholding the principles of fairness and equity, justice fosters a sense of accountability and maintains social order. It is the linchpin that binds ethics to action, translating moral ideals into tangible outcomes within the fabric of society. Where there's no justice, there's societal chaos.

6. Self-Reproach as the Path to Personal Growth

Self-reproach catalyzes personal introspection and growth, prompting individuals to confront their shortcomings and strive for improvement. Through honest self-reflection, one acknowledges past mistakes and commits to positive change, embarking on a journey toward inner peace and fulfillment. It is a crucial step toward self-awareness and emotional maturity, paving the way for greater harmony within oneself and with others.

Self-reproach is the unique domain where we don't function like God. He doesn't need self-reproach because He doesn't commit any errors. You can read about this theological issue in the book Mind-Body Problem Solved[11].

7. Forgiveness as the Key to Healing and Reconciliation

Forgiveness mends broken relationships and facilitates reconciliation, both with oneself and others. By letting go of resentment and embracing empathy, individuals release the burden of guilt and open the door to healing. It is a transformative process that requires courage and humility, fostering empathy and understanding in the face of adversity. Through forgiveness, human conduct can

11. https://theexplanation.com/read-content-of-mind-body-problem-solved-online/

transcend past grievances and forge a path toward greater compassion and unity.

In a word, the summary of applying the above seven traits of human conduct is *love*.

Human conduct is a complex interplay of dual tendencies, free will, behavior, ethical principles, justice, self-reflection, and forgiveness. By understanding and embracing these elements, individuals can navigate the intricacies of human behavior and contribute to a more harmonious and compassionate world. Transforming one's anxieties involves mature introspective reasoning of how we function and a compass to guide our life purpose.

14. Why Humans Excel: Unique Traits

Humans are exceptional. We are incomparable regarding integrating society (socialization) and managing our own and others' lives (rulership).

A recent study[1] was excited to announce that three crows can vocally count to four! After arduous training, the birds only succeeded in reaching four 40% of the time. Well, two to four-year-old kids can do that and so much more with simple teaching and triumph 100% of the time. Making the comparison that animals have the same intelligence as humans is ludicrous. They can accomplish some, even many, minimal tasks similar to humans; however, any parallels beyond that are exaggerated hyperbole.

Humans Possess Divine Essence, Neshama

1. https://www.smithsonianmag.com/smart-news/crows-can-count-up-to-four-like-human-toddlers-study-suggests-180984420/

Why so? Humans possess a portion of God's Neshama, while animals do not (Joshua 11:14). This Divine Essence breathed into humans at Creation (Genesis 2:7) confers on humans their humanity.

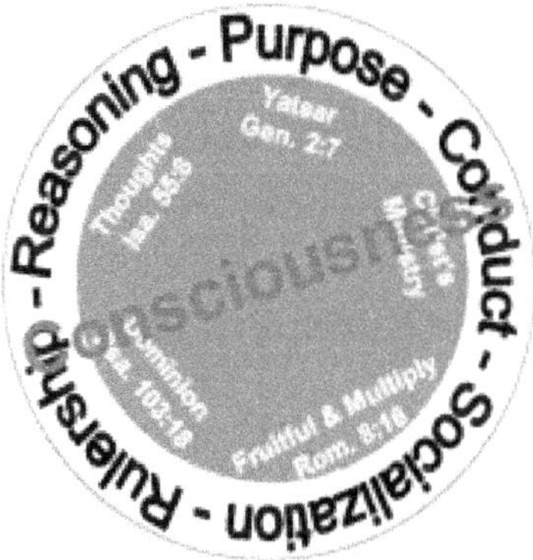

Figure 3. Bible-based five aspects of consciousness

Neshama is the equivalent of consciousness through which God endows every human being with His Image via five of His characteristics: reasoning (thoughts, Isa. 55:8), purpose (yatsar, Gen. 2:7), and conduct (Christ's Ministry); in this chapter, we broach socialization (Multiply, Rom. 8:16) and rulership (Dominion, Psa. 103:18).

Socialization – Family is the Foundation of Society

Socialization is the ability to be at ease by oneself and in the company of other people. *The Explanation* extensively describes this defining trait of humans[2] in *Audit of Humankind.* It crescendoes from individuals to communities, nations, and the world. Here is a series of articles about socialization[3].

2. https://theexplanation.com/social-relationships-puzzling-humans-love-hate/

3. https://theexplanation.com/social-relationships-puzzling-humans-love-hate/

- You are a Unique Individual among 8 Billion on Earth[4].
- Gender Equality, Gender Inequality, or Gender Compatibility?[5]
- Healthy Marriage, A Happy Twosome with Abundant Benefits[6].
- Family—The Cornerstone of Human Society[7].
- Nations Are Identified by Their Own Patriotic Ethnic Culture[8].

Chris Gardner – The Pursuit of Happyness

Let's illustrate socialization with the story of Chris Gardner's unwavering devotion to his young son, Christopher. Only humans care for their like in this way. Will Smith and his son played these roles in *Pursuit of Happyness*. It explored the depths of their bond, showcasing Chris's tireless efforts to care for and protect his son despite their overwhelming hardships; this is socialization.

Chris Gardner's dedication to his son is evident from the film's beginning. As they navigate a life of increasing instability, Chris's primary focus remains on providing for Christopher and ensuring his well-being. Chris goes to great lengths to shield his son from the harsh realities of their situation.

Night in a Restroom

One of the film's most memorable and heart-wrenching scenes is when Chris and Christopher are forced to spend the night in a subway

4. https://theexplanation.com/you-are-a-unique-individual-among-7-billion-on-earth/

5. https://theexplanation.com/gender-equality-gender-inequality-or-gender-compatibility/

6. https://theexplanation.com/healthy-marriage-a-happy-twosome-with-abundant-benefits/

7. https://theexplanation.com/family-the-cornerstone-of-human-society/

8. https://theexplanation.com/nations-identified-by-their-own-patriotic-ethnic-culture/

restroom. After being evicted from their apartment and having nowhere else to go, Chris leads his son into the restroom, locking the door behind them. In this small, cold space, Chris tries to create a sense of normalcy and security for Christopher. He imagines the bathroom floor as a cave and encourages Christopher to see it as an adventure, masking his despair and fear.

Chris's ability to maintain a facade of safety and fun in such a dire situation is a testament to his profound love and dedication. He uses a single sheet of toilet paper to make a pillow for his son, showing his resourcefulness and desire to provide even the smallest comforts. It speaks to the lengths Chris will go to protect his son, even when he feels vulnerable and defeated.

Another poignant scene that showcases Chris's devotion occurs when they are forced to move from one homeless shelter to another. Despite the shame and exhaustion, Chris maintains a brave face for his son. He engages Christopher in conversations about his dreams and aspirations, fostering a sense of hope and positivity. When Christopher expresses doubts or fears, Chris reassures him with unwavering confidence, emphasizing that their situation is temporary and that they will overcome it together. This emotional support is crucial in maintaining Christopher's sense of security and optimism.

Throughout the film, small, tender moments characterize Chris's relationship with Christopher, revealing the depth of their bond. Whether playing basketball together, helping Christopher with homework, or sharing a meal, these interactions are filled with love and care. Chris consistently prioritizes his son's emotional and physical needs, often at the expense of his own well-being. This selflessness is a cornerstone of their relationship and highlights the strength of their familial bond.

One of the film's most touching moments occurs when Chris finally secures a full-time position at the brokerage firm. Overwhelmed with emotion, he rushes to Christopher's daycare to share the news. As he embraces his son, the weight of their journey and the significance of this achievement are palpable. This moment is a culmination of Chris's tireless efforts and sacrifices, signifying a professional victory and a personal triumph in providing a stable future for his son—the ultimate socialization.

Rulership – Overseeing Oneself, People, and Possessions

Management is the human quality of overseeing one's life[9], including time, possessions, people, responsibilities, and anything else we are called to preside. Animal responsibilities are set by their species, and there's no deviation unless humans step in to alter that definitive path, like trying to teach crows to count.

With humans, at birth, we have no way of knowing what rulership path each person will carve out for themselves. Therein lies the responsibility of taking control of one's life, belongings, and the people with whom they will interact, regardless of supervisor or subordinate level.

The Explanation has developed this subject at length in *Audit of Humankind.*

- Human Needs, the Basics Each Person Should Expect[10].
- Inner Peace for Citizens is the Real Goal of Government[11].
- Peace of Mind, the Tranquil Result of Good Leadership[12].
- Prosperity for the Nation is Prosperity for Each Citizen[13].

9. https://theexplanation.com/human-rulership-responsibility-people-resources/

10. https://theexplanation.com/human-needs-basics-person-expect/

11. https://theexplanation.com/inner-peace-citizen-goal-government/

12. https://theexplanation.com/peace-mind-tranquil-result-leadership/

13. https://theexplanation.com/prosperity-nation-prosperity-citizen/

- Best Form of Government, Aiming for the Common Good[14].

Rulership of his possessions and eventual profession is one of the central elements of the film, with Chris Gardner's relentless effort to sell portable bone-density scanners. This venture plunges him into financial ruin but also serves as a symbol of his perseverance and ingenuity. Gardner's struggles with these devices provide crucial insights into his character and the overarching themes of resilience and hope.

Scanners to Setbacks

The film opens with Gardner investing his life savings in portable bone-density scanners, believing they represent a lucrative opportunity. These devices, however, prove challenging to sell due to their high cost and only marginal improvement over traditional X-rays. This miscalculation sets off a chain of financial hardships for Gardner, culminating in his eviction and descent into homelessness. Despite these challenges, Gardner's commitment to selling the scanners exemplifies his determination to turn his life around.

One of the most poignant scenes illustrating Gardner's dedication involves a beggar stealing one of his devices. Desperate to recover his investment, Gardner embarks on a frantic chase through the streets of San Francisco. It symbolizes Gardner's struggle against the relentless tide of misfortune that threatens to overwhelm him. When he finally catches up to the beggar, Gardner retrieves the scanner, demonstrating his tenacity and unwillingness to relinquish his dreams.

The bone-density scanners also represent Gardner's ability to solve problems creatively. In another significant scene, one of Gardner's scanners breaks, adding to his already overwhelming burdens. Instead of succumbing to despair, Gardner meticulously repairs the device,

14. https://theexplanation.com/best-form-government-aiming-common-good/

showcasing his resourcefulness and technical skill. This act of fixing the scanner is emblematic of Gardner's broader approach to life's challenges: when something breaks, whether it's a machine or his circumstances, he finds a way to fix it. This scene underscores his resilience and refusal to be defeated by adversity—rulership at its best.

The film also captures the mundane yet crucial aspects of Gardner's struggle with the scanners. Daily, he hauls these cumbersome devices through the city, presenting them to disinterested doctors and medical professionals. These scenes are repetitive, mirroring the monotonous grind of Gardner's daily life and emphasizing the sheer persistence required to keep going despite constant rejection. Every encounter with potential buyers tests Gardner's patience and optimism as he tirelessly demonstrates the scanners' features and benefits, hoping for just one sale to ease their financial strain.

Setbacks to Success

Despite the numerous setbacks, Gardner's breakthrough moment with the scanners is a testament to his perseverance and a turning point in his journey. In a crucial scene, he finally manages to sell one of the devices to a doctor, securing much-needed funds. Although small in the grand scheme of his financial woes, this victory represents a significant emotional boost. It reaffirms Gardner's belief in his ability to succeed and provides a glimmer of hope in an otherwise bleak situation.

Gardner had the traits of socialization and rulership and exercised them deftly. We have these human characteristics, including reasoning, purpose, and conduct, because God gave us neshama. It's like a blueprint that defines the mental structure of all humans. God-endowed consciousness makes us in His Image.

III. Ruach – Role in Humans

Ruach is the second spirit; it animates our neshama; together, these two spirits make us human.

Part III elaborates on HOW ruach operates in humans and its relationship to psychology.

Ruach is a crucial element in God's Plan. Spirit, God's Holy Spirit, is present as the Creation story develops in Genesis 1:2. The book *Mind-Body Problem Solved* devotes a couple of Parts with fourteen chapters to this fundamental and exciting subject.

For a complete understanding of how s/Spirit functions in Creation, animals, humans, and spiritual conversion, please refer to that book.

15. Two Spirits: Neshama and Ruach

Mental health points to the metaphysical beyond the body. So, what's apart from and together with the body? Two spirits reveal incredible human essence, according to the Bible.

We use two common terms daily: consciousness and mind, although science doesn't know what either of them is. It's time to reveal what they are and how they function. Only when you understand how a device operates optimally can you fine-tune it.

Humans have physical and mental specifications. We could list body parts and correlate them with their biological functions and nutritional needs. We know that the body gets sick if these needs are unmet. Identically, the human mental *parts* have nourishment essentials to meet their requirements for optimal functioning.

Unfortunately, the emphasis today is often on pills and potions, which cannot fix the causes of mental illness. What chemical therapy does is inhibit the physical part of the brain to try and control its expression of cognitive symptoms; this sidesteps the cause and only addresses the results, with all of the secondary effects added to the equation.

Mental Makeup – 2 Spirits

Only when we understand how the human mind functions can we know how to treat the causes of mental turmoil. The Bible reveals the composition of the human mind and how to treat it to reach the serenity many crave today.

All humans possess and are mentally animated by two, yes, two spirits. We have spent the past six chapters explaining what the first spirit is, the *breath* (neshama) of life. God infused a portion of His own Neshama into humans to make them *in His Image*, with His fundamental characteristics, which the Bible summarizes in five qualities: Reasoning, Purpose, Conduct, Socializing, and Ruling.

Let's use an analogy to show how neshama works. It's like an electrical grid built to serve five different structures: a house, an apartment building, a shopping center, a factory, and an industrial site. The wiring requirements differ based on each site's demands; this is your neshama's analogy. You have five separate and distinct traits that are related and intertwined. People live in houses or apartments, work in office buildings or industrial sites, and shop in shopping centers.

But here's the key to retain from this chapter: the entire electrical grid installed in the five structures cannot light up or operate any equipment unless connected to a power source. That origin is electricity. Similarly, neshama has to be activated by the second spirit, ruach.

Job 32:8

> But there is a *spirit* (H7307 – ruach) in man: and the *inspiration* (H5397 – neshama) of the Almighty gives them understanding (H995).

I realize this might be surprising information, but that's what God's Word states: 2 spirits, both from God. You can study the word *neshama* by searching the *Hebrew Concordance for H5397.* You'll find twenty-four verses with neshama, ten of which include *ruach*. Verify this at UnlockBibleMeaning.com[1] and read all the details in *Mind-Body Problem Solved*[2].

Job 27:3 (Job speaking)

> All the while my *breath* (H5397 – neshama) is in me, and the *spirit* (H7307 – ruach) of God is in my nostrils; (Sam: I wish that we be as wise a Job in our understanding that we possess two spirits).

Isaiah 42:5

> Thus says God the LORD, he that created the heavens, and stretched them out; he that spread forth the earth, and that which comes out of it; he that gives *breath* (H5397 – neshama) to the people upon it, and *spirit* (H7307 – ruach) to them that walk therein:

The English translation doesn't do justice to this last verse. I don't want to go off-course with the interpretation of this two spirits verse, but notice that *neshama* is more of a static spirit, given to the people, everyone on Earth; it is an innate characteristic. In contrast, *ruach* is associated with walking and is more active and dynamic, as we'll confirm in upcoming chapters.

---

1. https://unlockbiblemeaning.com/

2. *https://theexplanation.com/mind*

Look at the translations of these words to comprehend the immobile versus mobile contrast between these two spirits.

H5397

נְשָׁמָה n^e^shâmâh nesh-aw-maw'; from H5395 (נָשַׁם); a puff, i.e. wind, angry or vital breath, divine inspiration, intellect. or (concretely) an animal:

KJV – blast, (that) breath(-eth), inspiration, soul, spirit.

H7307

רוּחַ rûwach roo'-akh; from H7306 (רוּחַ); wind; by resemblance breath, i.e. a sensible (or even violent) exhalation; figuratively, life, anger, unsubstantiality; by extension, a region of the sky; by resemblance spirit, but only of a rational being (including its expression and functions):

KJV – air, anger, blast, breath, × cool, courage, mind, × quarter, × side, spirit(-ual), tempest, × vain, (whirl-) wind(-y).

Granted, these two spirits have similarities, but *neshama* is more of a noun, a thing, whereas ruach tends more to be a verb, an action. Another analogy I'd use is a blueprint that contains all the specifications and characteristics (neshama) of a house or bridge. However, energetic building and productive construction (ruach) will implement the plan.

The Two Spirits Work Together

Science cannot investigate or measure the two spirits. Therefore, it cannot ascertain how they function individually or together. That said, psychology has gathered much experience and can establish many theories about their functioning based on emotions, feelings, dreams, thoughts, behavior, the subconscious, and many other facets. This observation has given rise to a myriad of treatments, ranging from aromatherapy to hypnosis and electroshock to exposure therapy—some, unfortunately, with harmful results.

Before we can repair something, we must know what we're dealing with. With neshama and ruach, we have the grid on one side and the electricity supply on the other; in one sense, by themselves, each is useless and worthless. Only when you bring the two together is the real value expressed.

The Bible opens with a striking example of God's Neshama and Ruach, which we generally do not consider.

Genesis 1:2-3

> ... And the Spirit of God moved upon the face of the waters.
> And God said, Let there be light: and there was light.

God said is the outward expression of His *Neshama,* the vocalization of His Purpose (one of the five aspects of both God's and human consciousness). The *Spirit* of God is the Power by which He created light. The Purpose AND the Execution, the tandem of Neshama and Ruach creating together.

Psalm 33:6

> By the word of the LORD (God said) were the heavens made; and all the host of them by the *breath* (H7307 – Ruach) of his mouth.

This verse is an alternative way to express Genesis 1:1, where God made the heavens and earth. Throughout the Bible, we find similar expressions where we have the theoretical conception role of the *Neshama* and the active execution role of the *Ruach*. Unfortunately, we're not aware of this dichotomy of roles, and translations do not always help us.

> **Job 38:18** (God questions Job)
>
> Have you *perceived* (H995 – same Hebrew word as *understanding*, conveyed by God's Neshama in Job 32:8) the breadth of the earth? declare if you know it all.

This verse portrays the two spirits. Earth exists and has a diameter, a testimonial to its Creation by the power of God's Ruach. The question God asks Job pertains to *perception*: do you understand why the Earth has the width and breadth it does? Do you realize that the diameter of Earth influences our atmosphere, magnetic field, surface temperature, water, even the tectonic plates, and many other aspects of life we take for granted? The point is that God and humans must have specific traits to conceive monumental projects, which God possesses thanks to His Neshama. Humans can examine some aspects of God's Creation because they have a minimal portion of neshama.

God and humans can conceive, invent, imagine, execute, accomplish, and perform projects. We are in His image because we possess a portion of God's Neshama, our consciousness, and God's Ruach, our mind.

How Our Two Spirits Work Together

Here's another analogy to describe the two spirits: a five-page notepad and a pencil. At birth, each of us receives a five-page notepad. Each page represents one of the five aspects of consciousness: Reasoning, Purpose, Conduct, Socialization, and Rulership. That's our neshama spirit: it's innate, and each human automatically possesses it at birth. The pen represents the personal story we write daily on each page. That's our ruach spirit. We need the page to write on and the pen to write with. The two elements, the two spirits, are independent but also interdependent.

Mind Refreshed involves inspecting what we've written on our five notepad pages and:

1. Looking into our Reasoning, Purpose, Conduct, Socialization, and Rulership (our neshama consciousness) and recognizing what needs modifying or erasing.
2. Seeing what we should adjust or add; write with our ruach, spirit in humans, based on the correct principles?

When the five traits (neshama) are better aligned, and our effort (ruach) points in the right direction, we will improve our mental health and upgrade our lives; this book is all about how to do that.

16. Bible Ruach: Psychology 101

Humans are endowed with two spirits: neshama and ruach. Here's the ultimate guide to how they work together inseparably toward mental health and are known as consciousness and mind.

The Bible reveals that consciousness consists of five fundamental traits God and humans possess: the former in a Godly Realm and us in a human realm. Nonetheless, we have identical traits. How can *The Explanation* affirm this? Because the Bible states that we are in the likeness and image of God. Neshama, of which humans are the sole recipients (Genesis 2:7), confers on each of us five Godly Attributes: Reasoning, Purpose, Conduct, Socialization, and Rulership. These traits define the human constitution.

We are the only earthly beings to possess the duo neshama and ruach, two spirits that work intimately together. The Bible associates ruach with energy; let's reveal the extent of this second spirit. Remember, this is *spirit* with a small *s*, not the Holy Spirit; this is the spirit that animates ALL humans, past, present, and future. It also animates all animals, and in *Mind-Body Problem Solved*[1], Chapters 24-25, I address how it functions differently in them and humans because the latter alone possess neshama.

Zechariah 12:1

> The burden of the word of the LORD for Israel, says the LORD, which stretches forth the heavens, and lays the foundation of the earth, and *forms* (H3335, yatsar) the *spirit* (H7307) of man within him.

In Genesis 2:7, Yahveh Elohim *formed* (H3335) man; here, the same LORD *forms* (H3335) this ruach/spirit in humans. Just as He has a purpose for each human, He has a purpose for the spirit He formed within each of us (Numbers 16:22), along with the neshama He blew into humans. By the way, we now see the whole composition of humans—one dust body, including the brain, and two spirits, neshama and ruach.

These three elements, dust, neshama (consciousness), and ruach (mind), compose a soul, the living soul, in Genesis 2:7. This answers the $1.000.000 question 19 in the Preface: What is a soul?

Ruach = Power, Ability, Impel

Let's reveal the nature of this spirit and how it functions in connection with neshama.

Exodus 35:21

> And they (the Israelites) came, every one whose heart stirred him up, and every one whom his *spirit* (H7307) *made*

1. *https://TheExplanation.com/body*

> *willing* (H5068), and they brought the LORD'S offering to the work of the tabernacle of the congregation, and for all his service, and for the holy garments.

The spirit in humans *makes us willing;* it moves us to want to accomplish something with our lives. Haven't you wondered why humans want to conquer new heights? Why are we constantly pushing back our limits in all fields and walks of life? Because the ruach spurs and stimulates, the spirit moves and prods us, as the Biblical Hebrew for *made willing* (H5068) makes clear.

> **H5068**
>
> נָדַב nâdab naw-dab'; a primitive root; to impel; hence, to volunteer (as a soldier), to present spontaneously:
>
> KJV - offer freely, be (give, make, offer self) willing(-ly).

The ruach/spirit animates, enlivens, vitalizes, and energizes the neshama. It's the electricity in the circuit[2], the builders of the blueprint, the pen writing on the 5-page notepad.

2. https://theexplanation.com/2-spirits-neshama-ruach-reveal-human-essence/

Figure 4. Consciousness and Mind

The beige circular background symbolizes the ruach with the five elements of the neshama that it animates. This integrated spirit twosome is the foundational mental makeup of each human being. Mental health starts by focusing on this duo; we shall see how.

Ruach is the innate desire to progress and achieve what we set our hands to do. It's the ruach in us that is behind all the self-help programs available today. The Olympic motto epitomizes the purpose of the spirit in humans, placed in them by God; physically, for athletes, Citius—Altius—Fortius = Faster—Higher—Stronger in events like running or swimming, jumping or pole vaulting, weight-lifting, or wrestling.

Metaphysically or mentally, ruach/spirit/mind gives that same impetus to our neshama: compelled Reasoning, dynamic Purpose, striving Conduct, participative Socialization, and engaged Rulership—activating our inherent human qualities for our own and society's welfare and best interests.

Frankly, with the knowledge already exposed in *Mind Refreshed*, we know enough about humans to nurture mental health from the start of a new life. Let's reason (the 1st of the five traits of your neshama/consciousness); God made us in His Image by conferring Reasoning, Purpose, Conduct, Socialization, and Rulership on each human being. Second, He gave us the means to activate our consciousness to produce positive results. The way to nurture balanced human beings is to help them direct themselves (use the ruach) in the five areas of their consciousness (the ingrained Godly Elements) in line with God's Guidelines. That's the way to God's Image.

Ruach = Attitudes, Sentiments, Emotions

The ruach is the origin of our cognition, the mental action of acquiring knowledge and understanding through thought, experience, and the senses. Ruach is the power operating human mental processes, the invisible activities, including thinking, reasoning, and problem-solving. These processes form the basis of our actions, decisions, and feelings.

Joshua 2:11

> And as soon as we [the inhabitants of Jericho] had heard these things, our hearts did melt, neither did there remain any more *courage* (H7307) in any man, because of you: for the LORD your God, he is God in heaven above, and in earth beneath.

If I wanted to make a grammatical comparison between neshama and ruach, the former would be nouns and the latter verbs. The decision-making process of those in Jericho activated this absence of courage: their internal motivation process collapsed, and they lost their spirit, confidence, and hope.

Judges 8:3

> God has delivered into your hands the princes of Midian, Oreb and Zeeb: and what was I [the Judge, Gideon] able to do in comparison of you [the tribe of Ephraim]? Then their *anger* (H7307) was abated toward him, when he had said that.

Their ruach activated, and became *angry*. Gideon's words caused their anger-ruach to calm down. Our emotions are processes of the ruach in us.

Study *ruach* at UnlockBibleMeaning.com[3] and see how it causes variations of movement of our sentiments, affections, and feelings.

Ruach = Mind

In the following contexts, *ruach*, the human spirit, refers to the *mind*. In Genesis 26, the translators even used that word, which is correct.

Genesis 26:35

Which were a grief of *mind* (H7307) to Isaac and to Rebekah.

Genesis 41:8

And it came to pass in the morning that his *spirit* (H7307) was troubled; and he sent and called for all the magicians of Egypt, and all the wise men thereof: and Pharaoh told them his dream; but there was none that could interpret them to Pharaoh. (Sam: You can substitute *mind* for *spirit* in this verse. He was anxious.)

Genesis 45:27

And they told him [Jacob] all the words of Joseph (his son), which he had said to them: and when he saw the wagons which Joseph had sent to carry him, the *spirit* (H7307) of Jacob their father revived: (Sam: Jacob stopped brooding, good news brings peace of mind.)

Daniel 2:11

And in the second year of the reign of Nebuchadnezzar, Nebuchadnezzar dreamed dreams, wherewith his *spirit* (H7307) was troubled, and his sleep brake from him. (Sam: Do you see the active anxious mind?)

---

3. https://unlockbiblemeaning.com

Malachi 2:16

For the LORD, the God of Israel, says that he hates putting away: for one covers violence with his garment, says the LORD of hosts: therefore take heed to your *spirit* (H7307), that you deal not treacherously, (Sam: Our outward expression of violence starts with our minds ruminating, devising treachery)

In the New Testament, *Spirit* is *Pneuma*

In the New Testament, the spirit in humans is *pneuma* in Greek. Likewise, it is the active doing part of the neshama-ruach duo, synonymous with the *mind*.

Matthew 26:41

Watch and pray, that you enter not into temptation: the *spirit* (G4151) indeed is **willing**, but the flesh is weak. (Sam: the contrast of the mind's positive desires and the body's negative actions).

Mark 2:8

And immediately when Jesus **perceived** in his *spirit* (G4151) that they so reasoned within themselves, he said to them, Why reason you these things in your hearts? (Sam: Christ's mind knew the Pharisees were misusing their reasoning ability. Here, we see the combination of one of the characteristics of neshama, reasoning, coupled with its use by the mind, which in this case is equated with the heart).

John 4:23

> But the hour comes, and now is, when the true worshippers shall **worship** the Father in *spirit* (G4151) and in truth: for the Father seeks such to worship him. (Sam: true worship is not an external show, but in the mind that expresses itself outwardly, that's faith).

Romans 1:9

> For God is my witness, whom I **serve** with my *spirit* (G4151) in the gospel of his Son, that without ceasing I make mention of you always in my prayers; (Sam: Note *my spirit*, Paul is talking about his mind).

In all these verses, notice how the spirit, the mind, includes a verb, highlighted in bold: **willing**, **perceive**, **worship**, and **serve**, the perfect illustration of the mind applying the principles of God in the areas of Reasoning, Purpose, Conduct, Socialization, and Rulership. We now understand that *ruach* is *mind* and its relationship to neshama. It activates, energizes, powers, and stimulates consciousness.

IV. Bible Psychology for Everyone, Everywhere

Bible Psychology 101. God's Love and concern for all peoples' mental health. HOW God, humans, the Bible, and psychology assemble into one holistic ensemble.

17. Mental Health Begins in the Womb

Powerful influences are at work in your life months before you're born. And their effects are lifelong.

One element no one escapes is powerful influences on their life from the start. Mental illness is the number one health issue today. It involves each person troubled with such a dilemma, but it's much deeper than that. A sick family, company, environment, society, and nation potently influence each component.

Powerful Influences Before Birth

The National Institute of Health reports on powerful influences you succumbed to[1] before birth.

> The evidence suggests that there can be an increased risk to the future child if the mother feels stressed or has experienced early trauma. It is important to think and help beyond diagnosis.

1. https://www.ncbi.nlm.nih.gov/pmc/articles/PMC7491637/

> Several different types of prenatal stress for the mother have been shown to increase the risk of emotional, behavioral, and cognitive problems for the child and to play a causal role. Such stress in the mother includes her worry about the outcome of her pregnancy, her exposure to a raised level of daily hassles, to a natural or man-made disaster, and emotional cruelty or other forms of domestic abuse by her partner.

Mind Refreshed is not only an individual issue; it's a global societal phenomenon. As society goes, so go individuals. Today, powerful influences at play at societal and individual levels shape and either make or break us.

Internal and External Powerful Influences

Figure 5. Internal and External Influences

We now know that neshama/consciousness and ruach/mind are each person's mental workings regarding reasoning, purpose, conduct, socialization, and rulership capacities. Every second, we make choices in these five fundamental areas of our lives. Know that our personal decisions are based on strong internal and external pulls and pushes. The inner and outer circles illustrate some significant swaying windfalls, the decisive influences on your consciousness-mind duo.

The Effects of Internal Influences on Mental Health

Myriad factors shape your mental wellness, many deeply personal and internal. Numerous influences are present at birth because our physical and mental genealogy and societal effects all play a part in our prenatal formation. This primary period and the first few years of life are to nurture a baby's consciousness and mind. The critical periods[2] of a youngster are crucial for preventive mental health.

Here are some internal influences that characterize us from our start and throughout life.

Subconscious

In a deep layer of the ruach-mind, the subconscious is a powerful force that shapes mental health. It is an area where trances, hypnosis, deeper psychoanalysis, methods of meditation, manifestation, voices, and charlatan religion penetrate, especially those oriented to speaking in tongues and casting out demons. Hallucinogenic drugs and certain types of music that incite visions, out-of-body, and near-death experiences are controversial, powerful influences.

Dreams and nightmares are images, thoughts, and sensations that occur during sleep. They can indicate unresolved psychological issues, but we must handle interpretations carefully. Personal experiences, such as

---

2. https://theexplanation.com/critical-periods-when-babies-and-children-learn/

abuse, loss, accidents, or being in a war or natural disaster, both joyous and traumatic, can leave indelible marks on the subconscious.

If science does not understand consciousness, then subconsciousness should almost be off-limits; this is the most sensitive and potentially dangerous mental area each of us oversees. Avoid anything that causes loss of mind-control and diminishing or by-passing of your reasoning faculties; this is not the transformation of the mind that aligns with Biblical principles.

Emotions - Feelings

Emotions and feelings are powerful influences in our personal lives. Feelings, closely related to emotions, are the subjective experiences that arise from our thoughts and perceptions. While emotions such as joy, love, gratitude, anger, sadness, and fear are often automatic and physiological, feelings are the personal interpretation of those emotions.

Various methods tell us what's positive and negative and whether to express or repress them. Handle with care. The last section of this book will show you practical Biblical practices in line with reasoning, purpose, conduct, socialization, and rulership.

Talents

Recognizing and nurturing one's own and our offspring's talents and abilities provide a sense of purpose. Discovering one's talents and putting them to God-intended use is probably the greatest gift we can offer ourselves and society. Expanding horizons and giving people, from the earliest age possible, opportunities to explore their interests and test viable sound experiences opens minds to the wonders of planet Earth. Each must find his or her mindful way, which is what they want to devote their life to accomplishing.

It's a personal quest we should develop for ourselves and anyone life brings into our circle.

Intuition

Intuition, or the ability to understand something instinctively without needing conscious reasoning, plays a significant role in decision-making and mental health. More and more, authoritative figures advise listening to your heart or inner voice. What does your gut say?

It is as if you are your own life guide or you have an interior genie that aligns you with the starry truth. This book is Bible Psychology 101; it promotes God's celestial Truth, not our personal internal influences.

External Influences on Mental Health

Parents - Family

Parents are the primary caregivers and play a foundational role in the mental health of their children. The quality of parental care, emotional support, and the attachment style developed in early childhood significantly impact an individual's mental health. Positive parenting, characterized by warmth, responsiveness, and consistent discipline, fosters secure attachment and resilience in children.

Conversely, absent parenting, marked by neglect, abuse, or overprotection, can lead to a range of mental health issues, including anxiety, depression, and low self-esteem. The parental approach to stress and conflict resolution also models coping mechanisms for children, influencing their future mental health.

Extended family dynamics, including communication patterns and conflict resolution, shape an individual's psychological landscape. Supportive aunts and uncles promote a sense of belonging, but the presence of subversive issues within the family, such as substance or sexual abuse, increases the risk for other members.

Friends

Friends and peer groups are potent influences on mental health, particularly during adolescence and young adulthood. Positive friendships provide emotional support, companionship, and a sense of belonging, crucial for mental well-being.

Friends can also buffer against stress and help individuals navigate life challenges. However, negative influences, such as peer pressure, bullying, or exclusion, can have detrimental effects on mental health. Thus, the quality of friendships and social connections plays a crucial role in an individual's mental stability.

Society

Societal norms, values, and expectations shape mental health by influencing behavior, self-perception, and social interactions. Societal pressure to conform to specific standards of success, beauty, and behavior is ever-present. Whether based on race, gender, sexual orientation, or mental health status, discrimination and stigma exacerbate these issues by fostering feelings of alienation and worthlessness.

Conversely, a society that promotes inclusivity, acceptance, and mental health awareness can enhance well-being and reduce the prevalence of mental health disorders.

Country

The country in which one lives can profoundly impact mental health through its political stability, economic conditions, and social policies. Countries with high levels of political instability, conflict, or corruption often see higher rates of mental health issues due to insecurity.

On the other hand, countries with robust social support systems and effective public health policies tend to have better overall mental health outcomes.

Economic and Health Situations

Economic stability and access to healthcare are critical determinants of mental health. Economic hardship, unemployment, and financial stress are major risk factors for mental health disorders. Health situations, including chronic illness or disability, are challenges, while access to quality healthcare can mitigate these effects.

Culture and Religion

Culture influences values, practices, and even stigma related to mental well-being. Religion and spirituality can provide significant benefits, including a sense of purpose, community, and coping mechanisms for dealing with life's challenges. However, rigid or punitive religious doctrines can also contribute to guilt, anxiety, and exclusion.

Schooling

Schooling and education significantly affect mental health by shaping cognitive development, self-esteem, and social skills. Positive school environments that provide supportive relationships, academic encouragement, and opportunities for personal growth foster mental well-being. Conversely, negative experiences such as academic pressure, bullying, or lack of support can lead to stress and anxiety.

Internal and external influences on our mental health are and will always be present. God gave us the two spirits, neshama and ruach, to exercise mental capacity to the best of our ability. There are a zillion promoted ways to do so, and we have free will to choose what we desire.

Along with God-given consciousness and mind, God gave the proven method for sound mental health for all humankind, believers and non-believers alike. We shall see the compass direction to take and the guardrails to keep within to nurture sane minds and heal mental illness.

18. God's Love Heals Non-Believers

Many believers think God condemns non-believers to Hell. That idea is light-years from the truth. God's Love encompasses the mental health of each human.

God yearns for non-believers to savor mental health. Here's conclusive Biblical proof gleaned from the Biblical Hebrew. In the Garden of Eden, God expounded on Adam and Eve's life **purpose**: **socialization**, **rulership**, and how to **conduct** themselves by exercising their free will to **reason** and decide. These are the five fundamentals of consciousness that you and I exert every second of every day of our lives.

In the last chapter, we saw that all humans are subject to internal and external influences on their minds. How we manage our minds and these influences is the crux of mental health. When Adam and Eve ate from the forbidden Tree, they had a mind-makeover; they transformed into non-believers. Instead of accepting God's Word, they switched to their own wisdom. That's the definition of a non-believer. Despite that, God did not abandon them.

Clothed in Coats of Skins

A strange event occurs immediately before the couple's expulsion from the Garden of Eden. The narrative turns to clothing; why? The figurative profoundness of Biblical Hebrew reveals God's Love for all humankind, regardless of belief, race, gender, or any other criteria. He's concerned with the mental health of all non-believers.

> **Genesis 3:21**
>
> To Adam also and to his wife did the LORD God make *coats* (H3801) of *skins* (H5785), and *clothed* (H3847) them.
>
> Here's Strong on clothed in the verse above[1].
>
> **H3847**
>
> לָבַשׁ lâbash law-bash'; or לָבֵשׁ; a primitive root; properly, wrap around, i.e. (by implication) to put on a garment or clothe (oneself, or another), literally or figuratively:
>
> KJV - (in) apparel, arm, array (self), clothe (self), come upon, put (on, upon), wear.

At the beginning of *Agony of Humankind,* we discussed clothing in the context of the man's and the woman's nakedness[2]. Please revise the information at the link. To summarize, the figurative usage of clothing is dirty and clean clothing represents sinful and righteous living.

Clothing Represents the State of Mind - Mental Health

Figuratively, clothing points us to a *frame of mind* and a way of acting—conduct. God made Adam and Eve, non-believers, *coats*

1. https://UnlockBibleMeaning.com

2. https://theexplanation.com/adam-and-eve-naked-possessing-spiritual-wisdom/

(H3801)—to protect their muddied minds despite their new sinful way of thinking.

H3801

כְּתֹנֶת k^ethôneth keth-o'-neth; or כֻּתֹּנֶת; from an unused root meaning to cover (compare H3802 (כָּתֵף)); a shirt:

KJV - coat, garment, robe.

H3802

כָּתֵף kâthêph kaw-thafe'; from an unused root meaning to clothe; the shoulder (proper, i.e. upper end of the arm; as being the spot where the garments hang); figuratively, side-piece or lateral projection of anything:

KJV - arm, corner, shoulder(-piece), side, undersetter.

In the New Testament, the Apostle Paul refers to upper clothing: "...having on the breastplate of righteousness" (Ephesians 6:14). God dresses non-believers in protective garments.

Think about this historic moment: the commencement of a new civilization. They'd just sinned and needed new shielded clothing to survive in their unfamiliar world.

In their NEW LOCATION, Eden, Adam and Eve needed the know-how and rules to play and win at socialization, rulership, and mental health.

God's Clothing is *Nakedness in Blindness*

In the Garden of Eden, God's Dwelling, God's SPIRITUAL rules apply. However, different rules apply outside of Eden, mainly where

Given their diminished mental state, which characterized Adam and Eve and all of humankind now, God gave them NEW and DIFFERENT rules based on their spiritual blindness. Non-believers received a new code of ethics based on their human wisdom.

God clothed Adam and Eve; figuratively, this is instruction on how to lead their lives in the new world correctly (*nakedness*) and maintain mental health as non-believers (*blindness*).

Who Are These Coats of Skins For?

Adam and Eve represent non-believers who move into a new era in Eden. Later, Cain, representing the entirety of humanity, is sent out of Eden into *this world* (John 14:30). The coats of skins are for non-believers. They represent the new rules of life. The Bible doesn't use the term rules. Instead, we find vocabulary like *laws*, *commandments*, *judgments*, and *statutes*.

1. Cain had commandments (Gen. 4:5-7).
2. During Noah's days, God "saw that the wickedness of man was great in the earth" (Gen. 6:5). The population had put off the coats of skins. There's similar wickedness in Sodom (Gen. 13:13).

Old Testament Israel was a WORLDLY Nation

God chose the people of Israel, descendants of Abraham, as a special people. But what most Bible readers know but don't consider is they were just as DISobedient as any other nation. They are the prime example of non-believers, being blind and clothed in coats of skins:

1. After the Exodus, God officialized the Ten Commandments (the coat of skins) for the nation of Israel AND all the non-Israelites that accompanied them on departure from Egypt.

This observation means the Commandments are for ALL people.
2. In Deuteronomy, God *updated* the law (modified their style of coats) for their new environment in the Promised Land.

These **commandments represent the coat of skins** that a REBELLIOUS nation was to follow to be under God's Protection and benefit from His blessings, including mental health. Today, that SAME clothing is valid for Israel's descendants and the entire world.

Deuteronomy 4:30-31

When you are in tribulation, and all these things are come upon you, **even in the *latter* days**, if you turn to the LORD your God, and shall be obedient to his voice; For the LORD your God is a merciful God...

God wants His UNconverted nation to maintain a balanced spiritual and physical life. The inhabitants are to recognize and respect His commandments regarding socialization and rulership, which I will expand on.

The Coats of Skins are for All Non-Believers Worldwide

God did not give the Ten Commandments code of ethics solely for Israel's sake. It was for the WHOLE WORLD. Meditate on this generally overlooked following passage; it's the key to understanding how God works with non-believers. Israel was to be a BEACON nation. The LIGHT shining in the dark, the coats of skins projecting GOD'S RIGHTEOUS statutes, judgments, and law (see verse 8 below). Israel and ALL nations could see God and His code of ethics leading to peace of mind and prosperity.

Deuteronomy 4:5-9

> 5 Behold, I have taught you statutes and judgments, even as the LORD my God commanded me, that you should do so in the land whither you go to possess it.
>
> 6 Keep therefore and do them; for this is your wisdom and your *understanding* (coats of skins) in the sight of the nations, which shall hear all these statutes, and say, Surely this great nation is a *wise and understanding* people (mentally healthy).
>
> 7 For what nation is there so great, who has God so nigh to them, as the LORD our God is in all things that we call upon him for?
>
> 8 And what nation is there so great, that has statutes and judgments so righteous as all this *law* (to protect their minds), which I set before you this day?
>
> 9 Only take heed to yourself, and keep your soul diligently, lest you forget the things which your eyes have seen, and lest they depart from your heart all the days of your life: but teach them your sons, and your sons' sons;

Only when individuals and a nation are ready to accept God's Way of Life for non-believers and adjusted to MODERN living, as we'll see, will God intervene to bless that nation. Study the examples of King Josiah (2 Kings 22-23) and Jonah sent to Nineveh, which was NOT an Israelite nation but benefited from repenting and putting on God's Coats of Skins.

God's Ways, when followed, lead to mental health for all people then and now.

19. Bible Psychology: Mental Health Tips

The Bible is not a psychology book, but God is the Creator of humankind, and Bible psychology—the Divine Guide from fundamentals to mental health mastery for all.

Two Greek words compose Bible *psychology*: *psyche,* meaning *consciousness*, and *logos*, meaning *study*. In English, we use *psyche* with other significations such as *spirit* and *soul.*

Consciousness and Mind

At the base of the mind is consciousness. Genesis 2:7 defines this as the neshama, the understanding and awareness God places in each human being. Consciousness is present from birth and is the fundamental makeup of every human. Neshama identifies what a human is[1].

1. https://theexplanation.com/astonishing-meaning-what-it-means-to-be-human/

Each human possesses the five elements: Reasoning, Purpose, Conduct, Socialization, and Rulership. Interaction is permanent and continuous from the start of life to the end. The circle in the image above portrays the presence of these five traits.

The mind, the spirit-ruach encompasses this circle on all sides; the neshama and ruach are inseparable. *The Explanation* has already clarified that the mind is ruach[2], the spirit in (hu)man(s) (Job 32:8) placed there by God. So, if we want to use the term spirit, that is no problem. This power activates, mobilizes, triggers, switches on, calls on, and stimulates; specifically, the spirit in humans energizes our consciousness, the neshama.

The mind is continuously active regarding consciousness. Bible psychology involves both working together.

Everything the mind does, thinking mentally or accomplishing physically, is associated with the five elements of consciousness. For instance, take *purpose*. Each person thinks about their purpose in life; some, even many, depending on culture and other circumstances, have no say in their life destiny. Others may follow their whims. Many might not know and take time to figure it out. Based on their talents and likes, some might know at an early age what they want to accomplish and establish a plan to reach that goal.

All the thinking, hesitation, fortitude, planning, effort, or not to do something with one's life is mind activity around the conscious concept that humans have a *purpose*.

What about the Brain?

You've noticed that whereas practically all psychology books focus on the brain and neuroscience, *Mind Refreshed* has not broached this

2. https://theexplanation.com/mental-mind-fabulous-activity-of-consciousness/

subject. Genesis 2:7 says God formed man from the dust of the earth. That includes the visible, measurable brain. Neshama, consciousness, and ruach, mind, are spirits; hence, they are invisible and outside the material body. The physical brain is the transducer that converts mind waves to brainwaves and vice-versa. It allows our mind to interact with our body to transmit our physical sensations (from our five senses) to our non-physical thoughts and vice versa.

The brain is an essential part of our body, but emotions, thoughts, feelings, and so on do not originate there. Please read The Human Brain: Its Surprising Agile Role in Body and Mind[3] in *Mind-Body Problem Solved* for a full explanation.

Internal and External Influences

Our consciousness and minds are subject to every influence around us. So, we need to add these effects to the definition of the psychology diagram. Each person has intuition, personal experiences, subconscious activity, dreams, emotions, and feelings to different degrees. These are powerful because they are vivid personal events affecting our minds and bodies. They are genuine and authentic. There's no point in denying them or trying to convince someone of their non-existence.

3. https://theexplanation.com/the-human-brain-role-in-consciousness-and-mind/

Figure 6. Internal and External Influences

There are external events over which we have no or little control. We are born into conditions beyond our control. The first influence we undergo is socialization. Do parents, mother, and father cuddle us? Does Mom breastfeed us? Is Dad present, and does he play with us? These simple questions have everlasting effects on babies to be, children to be, adults to be, and the next generation of leaders responsible for the generation of babies after us. And the circle goes round and round.

This parenting is the nurture aspect of our human composition that each bears and, in adolescence and adulthood, brings into our decisions, relationships, and way of life. These influences can be damaging, neutral, or positive. We all have a personal mixture of these traits representing our personality and character. This whole combination of components makes us an individual like no other on this planet.

The combination of all these influences on our consciousness and mind gives rise to the state of our mental health. When we control and master these elements in line with proper Reasoning, Purpose,

Conduct, Socialization, and Rulership, we benefit from mental health. When these conditions are non-existent or out of kilter, when Bible psychology is out of focus, we can suffer from mental ill-health.

Psychology 101 - Its Biblical Meaning

Let's look at the meaning of the two Greek words that compose psychology: *psycho* and *logos*. Please understand an important point. Practically nobody knows that breath is neshama in Genesis 2:7. Nobody besides *The Explanation* has revealed that neshama is the equivalent of consciousness. I'm not saying this to boast because God revealed this. I'm stating it because nobody has this theology of the Old Testament. So, when we come to New Testament *psycho*, we can't expect any better theology or translations; this is the origin of total confusion.

Psyche

The number of translations in Hebrew and Greek reveals the difficulty with the concepts of *spirit* and *mind*. The translation *consciousness* is not to be found anywhere in the Bible.

In Hebrew, *mind* is translated by the words *zimma* (plan – H2154), *yetzer* (purpose – H3336), *lev* (heart – H3820), *nefesh* (soul – H5315), *peh* (mouth – H6264), and *ruach* (spirit – H7307).

There are 15 Greek words rendered *mind* or derivatives like *bring to mind*. The principal words are *noos* (understanding – G3563), and *phroneo* (understanding – G5426). The primary Greek word is *psuche* (G5990), from which we get *psycho*, the first part of *psycho*logy. It appears 109 times and is rendered *mind* a mere 3x, *life* 40x, and *soul* 58x. Do you see the confusion?

G5590

ψυχή psuchē psoo-khay'; From G5594; breath that is (by implication) spirit abstractly or concretely (the animal sentient principle only; thus distinguished on the one hand from G4151 which is the rational and immortal soul; and on the other from G2222 which is mere vitality even of plants: these terms thus exactly correspond respectively to the Hebrew [H5315] [H7307] and [H2416]:

KJV – heart (+ -ily), life, mind, soul + us + you.

The following verse points us in the right direction of understanding.

Philippians 1:27

Only let your conversation be as it becomes the gospel of Christ: that whether I come and see you, or else be absent, I may hear of your affairs, that you stand fast in one *spirit* (G4151 pneuma), with one *mind* (G5590 psuche) striving together for the faith of the gospel;

We have no difficulty understanding the English translations *spirit* and *mind*. However, I would offer you an alternative: *ruach* (pneuma – spirit) and *neshama* (psuche – consciousness). Do a study at UnlockBibleMeaning.com[4], find G5590 (psuche), display all the verses using *Greek Concordance for G5590*, and substitute the translation *consciousness* for *psuche*.

Paul tells the Philippians to think (with their minds-pneuma) like Christ based on their five-fold God-given consciousness (psuche). In other words, they must think as Christ thinks about Reasoning, Purpose, Conduct, Socialization, and Rulership; they should be God-Bible aligned.

4. https://unlockbiblemeaning.com

Logos

In dictionary terms, *logos, the logy* of Bible psycho*logy, means a study or research of consciousness.* To understand the confusion that reigns in the study and research of this subject, I suggest you peruse this article[5]. I leave you with a partial quote: "...there is still a lot of difference of opinion concerning what the exact nature of mind is, and various competing definitions have been proposed." A similar article about consciousness[6] states, "Opinions differ about what exactly needs to be studied or even considered consciousness." That says it all.

Logos has other meanings, like *logic* or reasoned discourse, and a *logo* that identifies a company or organization. In Biblical terms, *Logos* is of the utmost importance, translated as the *Word* and used as the name of God (Revelation 19:13) and Scripture (Luke 8:11).

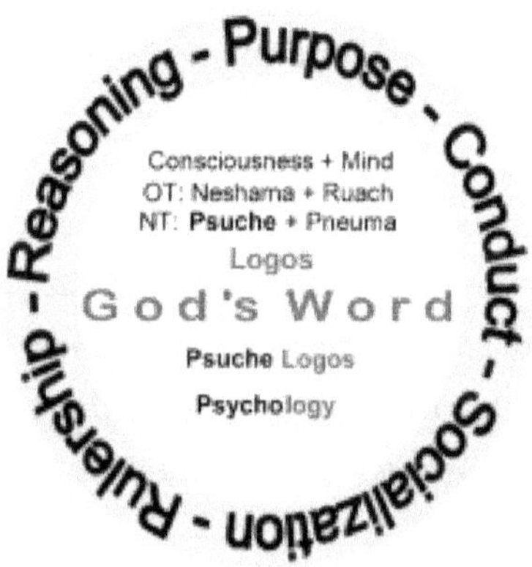

Figure 7. Psychology = Psuche + Logos = Neshama + God's Word

Logos means sound reasoning and proper science dealing with the rules and processes used in accurate thinking and reasoning—the logic,

5. https://en.wikipedia.org/wiki/Mind

6. https://en.wikipedia.org/wiki/Consciousness

reflection, and meditation that come from God's Word. So, the definition of *Bible psychology* is NOT about *humankind's research of the psyche*; Bible psychology is the *psuche* and *pneuma* under the benevolence of God's *Logos*.

From Creation, we have neshama and ruach, with God informing Adam and Eve how to use them. In the next chapter, we shall see the Old Testament teachings on mental health and well-being for ALL humans, which we will see are still valid today.

The definition of *Bible psychology*:

> **God's Word applied to the neshama and ruach.**

The Logos is the basis for mastering our psuche and pneuma.

The diagram reveals the *psuche-consciousness* and the *pneuma-mind* under the caring umbrella of God's *Logos, God's Word*: practical, efficient Bible psychology.

From the confusion of science and philosophy, we come to the simplicity of Christ. Frankly, Bible Psychology 101 is not rocket science. We now know what a human is and how we can function for optimum mental health.

20. Divine Design: Mental Health Blueprint

Just like a skyscraper or a plane, when God formed man, it required norms for quality and durability for optimal mental health.

Then, ongoing maintenance specifications are needed to keep it functioning optimally. These same principles apply to planet Earth and when the Creator formed man, its human inhabitants. But, when proper upkeep is not met, water seeps in, as does mental ill-health.

Understand that God has wisdom and knows what He did when He formed man to possess and maintain mental health (Proverbs 3:19-20).

Luke 14:28-30

28 For which of you, intending to build a tower, sits not down first, and counts the cost, whether he have sufficient to finish it?

> 29 Lest haply, after he has laid the foundation, and is not able to finish it, all that behold it begin to mock him,
>
> 30 Saying, This man began to build, and was not able to finish.

God has taken into account all scenarios. Just as establishing construction requirements for a building, the architect must consider earthquake, wind, and soil conditions. When flying through hurricane winds for scientific purposes, a plane must be built with tolerance and resilience to withstand extreme pressure and hold together to protect its precious cargo.

God Formed Man and Woman for Prosperity and Mental Health

When God formed man and Earth, He did the same. Humans have a tolerance for altitudes, temperatures, and air intake; we live in the tropics and the Arctic. Imagine if someone took one puff on a cigarette or a sugar-laced soft drink and dropped dead. We have to do a lot of misuses before the cogs get clogged, and we come to a standstill. That's physical health. Well, the same applies to mental health.

God formed man and woman with tolerant consciousnesses and minds. We can feed our mental faculties an awful lot of junk ideas, drugs, phony practices, fake news, and lies before there are signs of a downward spiral from mental equilibrium to instability. However, there is a pivot point where this happens, and the pendulum begins to swing in the opposite direction.

Let's look at the Biblical narrative and follow this sad story of how God formed man to stand firm mentally and why we've stumbled, not to say tumbled, into mental ill-heath.

Genesis 2:7

> And the LORD God *formed* (Sam: H3335[1] with the required qualities, durability, and resilience toward the purpose of stable mental health) man of the dust of the ground, and breathed into his nostrils the breath of life; and man became a living soul.

God put the mentally healthy couple in an ideal environment, which they disdained, succumbing to the Adversary. They ate of the forbidden Tree of the Knowledge of Good and Evil. God told them they'd have sorrow (Gen. 3:16-17) but clothed them with coats of skins[2] in the most unusual event before expulsing them into Eden and their descendants into this world.

We've already seen that the coats of skins represent a new nakedness adapted to their spiritual blindness[3]. Not the wisdom and righteousness associated with the Garden of Eden but the wisdom and righteousness involved with living in their new environment, *this world.*

John 8:23

> And he [Jesus] said to them, You are from beneath; I am from above: you are of *this world*; I am not of *this world.*

Christ is from the Garden of Eden, spiritual righteousness. This world is human righteousness, which we'll define in a minute. There's a definite distinction between Christ's white robes and the coats of skins God formed for man to wear in this world, which represent the code of ethics humans are to don

---

1. https://UnlockBibleMeaning.com
2. https://theexplanation.com/non-believers-acquire-mental-health-gods-love/
3. https://theexplanation.com/non-believers-acquire-mental-health-gods-love/

Do Good

I want to warn you that we are about to broach a very practical subject that is theologically, totally misunderstood. Since you're hearing this for the first time, you'll probably need to read it a few times and do some study and meditation. It revolves around the *coats of skins* God dressed His man and woman with. What is this *code of ethics*?

> **Jeremiah 4:22**
>
> For my people is foolish, they have not known me; they are sottish children, and they have none understanding: they are *wise to do evil*, but to *do good* they have no knowledge.

The prophet Jeremiah is talking about God's degenerate, disobedient descendants of Abraham, Isaac, and Jacob, the Israelites; this is a spiritually UNconverted people to whom God did NOT offer spiritual conversion as He does AFTER Christ's Death and Resurrection. Notice, these Israelites, AND the rest of the world population, then and NOW, are wise, but to *do evil not good.*

What evil, and especially, what good is God referring to?

> **Genesis 2:8-9**
>
> 8 And the LORD God planted a garden eastward in Eden; and there he put the man whom he had formed.
>
> 9 And out of the ground made the LORD God to grow every tree that is pleasant to the sight, and good for food; the tree of life also in the midst of the garden, and the tree of **knowledge of good** and *evil.*

Here's the theological error. We look at this Tree of the Knowledge of Good and Evil ONLY as an evil tree. That is not entirely the case. The truth is this Tree contains the *knowledge of good*. What is that? It is the good that human wisdom should be able to RECOGNIZE and DO! The coats of skins portray this *good*; this is human righteousness.

The fact is humans have the wisdom to know we should not murder, lie, steal, commit adultery, get drunk and drive, take drugs, and blow our minds. Most people lean toward the good with some evil. Some are a mixture, while others, a minority, are on the evil side. Humans are wise enough to reason what's good, do a minimum in that area, and be conscious of it.

Romans 2:13-15

13 For not the hearers of the law are just before God, but the doers of the law shall be justified.

14 For when the Gentiles, which have not the law (Sam: God's Old Testament law, fundamentally the Ten Commandments), do by nature (Sam: human wisdom) the things contained in the law, these, having not the law, are a law unto themselves (Sam: they've eaten of the Tree of the Knowledge of Good and Evil and decide for themselves what the laws are):

15 Which shew the work of the law written in their hearts (Sam: they choose the *good*), their conscience also bearing witness, and their thoughts the mean while accusing or else excusing one another (Sam: human judgment with human wisdom);

The *knowledge of good and evil* is human wisdom and righteousness. People devise their own codes of ethics, and their knowledge can be, and in many cases is, in agreement with God's code of ethics; this is the *coats of skins* God dressed His man and woman with.

Results of Human Wisdom Applying the Good

One of the repetitive themes throughout the Old Testament, whether with God's people or everyone else, is the continual emphasis on *choosing to do good.* The first words to Adam are what to do with the two Trees: choose good. God's advice to Cain is to do good toward his brother. Through Noah, a preacher of righteousness (2 Peter 2:5), God wanted the world population to do good. All this *doing good* is the *good* of the Tree of the Knowledge of *Good* and Evil.

It is essential to realize that this righteousness preached by Noah, or devised by human wisdom, is not the spiritual righteousness of converted Christians in the New Testament. It is taking off the fig leaves and putting on the coats of skins, using one's human wisdom to grasp that the laws God gave the people, first and foremost the Ten Commandments, are the basis of the coats of skins. Whether it be Cain, Noah's epoch, Sodom & Gomorrah, the Exodus, or Deuteronomy, and the entry into the Promised Land, all the instruction was to help people use their human wisdom to apply fundamental laws for their and others' good.

When applied, this wisdom had definite promises that are still valid today. Study the Old Testament for this theme.

> **Deuteronomy 30:9-19**
>
> 9 And the LORD your God will make you plenteous in every work of your hand, in the fruit of your body (Sam: and the fruit of your mind with mental health), and in the fruit of your cattle, and in the fruit of your land, for good: for the

> LORD will again rejoice over you for good, as he rejoiced over your fathers:
>
> 10 If you shall hearken to the voice of the LORD your God, to keep his commandments and his statutes which are written in this book of the law, and if you turn to the LORD your God with all your heart, and with all your soul.
>
> 11 For this commandment which I command you this day, it is not hidden from you, neither is it far off.
>
> 14 But the word is very nigh to you, in your mouth, and in your heart, that you may do it. (Sam: represented by the coats of skins)
>
> 15 See, I have set before you this day life and *good*, and death and *evil*; (Sam: The Tree of Good and Evil is in front of each of us)
>
> 19 I call heaven and earth to record this day against you, that I have set before you life and death, blessing and cursing: therefore choose life (Sam: the *good* of the Tree), that both you and your seed may live (Sam: a message about parenting and nurturing mental health in our children):

Mental disease is not a fatality; it's a national and personal CHOICE. God formed man, all of us, to *do good* and be blessed with mental stability. If we *choose evil*, mental ill-health is inevitable.

In the following chapter, we shall focus on the Bible's code of ethics for humankind in this 21st Century, the sound code that leads to mental health for all.

21. 21st Century Proverbs Commandments

Religion considers the 10 Commandments from a theological, Testament, Covenant, or doctrinal perspective. What about the practical?

Everyone asks the theological question, "Are the 10 Commandments still valid today?" That in itself is a negative proposition. Here's what we should be asking: Why did God generate and give humans the 10 Commandments? What's His perspective? How are the 10 Commandments relevant to improved mental health today?

Short History of the *Commandments*

They were present in the Garden of Eden through Cain, Noah, Nimrod, Abraham, and his descendants. God formalized the 10 Commandments to the 12-tribe nation of Israel and the mixed multitude on Mount Sinai after the Exodus. Forty years later, in Deuteronomy, Moses reiterated God's 10 Commandments and many others as the specific recipe for living prosperously and healthily (in body and mind) in the Promised Land.

Then, umpteen ups and downs followed as the leadership and people waxed and waned regarding the 10 Commandments. When they obeyed, blessings ensued, while disobedience brought hardship and catastrophe. Finally, extreme disobedience culminated in God allowing the entire northern ten tribes of Israel to be taken captive by the Assyrians around 720 BC, and about 120 years later, the same calamity on the two remaining tribes, Judah and Benjamin, along with the destruction of the Temple in Jerusalem.

Solomon Published Wisdom Books

During this tumultuous period, there are a few brief, glorious periods of righteousness. One is King David and the beginning of his son's reign, Solomon. One of the highlights of that era is Solomon's prayer to God.

> **1 Kings 3:7-12**
>
> 7 And now, O LORD my God, you have made your servant king instead of David my father: and I am but a little child: I know not how to go out or come in.
>
> 8 And your servant is in the midst of your people which you have chosen, a great people, that cannot be numbered nor counted for multitude.
>
> 9 Give therefore your servant **an *understanding* (H8085, hearing, obedient, publish...) heart to *judge* (H8199, reason, rule...) your people, that I may *discern* (H995) between good and bad (Sam: the Tree of good and evil)**: for who is able to judge this your so great a people?

> 10 And the speech pleased the Lord, that Solomon had asked this thing.
>
> 11 And God said to him, Because you have asked this thing, and have not asked for yourself long life; neither have asked riches for yourself, nor have asked the life of your enemies; but have asked for yourself understanding to discern judgment;
>
> 12 Behold, I have done according to your words: lo, I have given you a *wise* and an *understanding* (H995) heart; so that there was none like you before you, neither after you shall any arise like to you.

Read the entire context at UnlockBibleMeaning.com[1]. The deep significance of this discussion has evaded us; here it is. Solomon wants to know how to govern the nation to benefit their prosperity in every way possible, including their mental health.

We must meditate on God's Gift to accomplish Solomon's desire: a wise and *understanding heart*; this is what neshama does precisely: "The *inspiration* (neshama) of the Almighty gives them *understanding*" (H995, Job 32:8). We've defined neshama as consciousness[2], composed of five vital traits: Reasoning, Purpose[3], Conduct, Socialization[4], and Rulership[5].

God gave Solomon THE understanding of HOW TO govern UNconverted people (the nation of Israel, and by extension ALL

---

1. https://UnlockBibleMeaning.com
2. https://theexplanation.com/human-consciousness-why-how-we-got-breakthrough/
3. https://theexplanation.com/mystery-of-human-conduct-origin-wonders-woes/
4. https://theexplanation.com/socialization-rulership-humanity-excels-animals/
5. https://theexplanation.com/socialization-rulership-humanity-excels-animals/

people) in these five domains so they'd benefit the most from their life in this world.

God poured out on Solomon the keys to mental health. He lived, experienced, and wrote profusely about Reasoning, Purpose, Conduct, Socialization, and Rulership, and how to maintain optimum mental health for ALL humankind.

> **1 Kings 4:30, 32**
>
> 30 And Solomon's wisdom excelled the wisdom of all the children of the east country (Sam: the origin of Oriental Philosophy, Buddhism, mindfulness, and other non-Biblical practices), and all the wisdom of Egypt.
>
> 32 And he spake three thousand proverbs: and his songs were a thousand and five.

Wisdom Books and The Writings

Solomon's book of Proverbs contains about 800 Proverbs, and we have the Song of Solomon; most of his writing is not in the Canon, The Bible. His writings are among the Wisdom Writings, one of the three parts of the Bible: *The Writings*, *Torah*, and the *Prophets*. Christ summed it up in Luke 22:44, "These are the words which I spake to you, while I was yet with you, that all things must be fulfilled, which were written in the Law of Moses (Torah, Law, Pentateuch), and in the Prophets (Neviim), and in the Psalms (Ketuvim, Writings), concerning me."

The Writings also contain Ecclesiastes (wisdom for *depression*), Lamentations (wisdom for *grief*), Ruth (wisdom for *racial* issues), and Esther (wisdom about *God's Justice*). *The Writings* include the last books written in the Old Testament: Ezra, Nehemiah, and Chronicles.

I want you to grasp that this Section is the ultimate Word of God for the UNconverted. Understand that there are only two groups of people in *this world*[6]:

1. The **converted:** God's people who eat from the *Tree of Life* through the Holy Spirit.
2. The **UNconverted**: ALL people not called at this time, who live IN THIS WORLD, who eat from the *Tree of Good and Evil*, and who should do the Good.

Please comprehend the extent of the UNconverted of THIS WORLD. Those are the people for whom Solomon wrote the book of Proverbs, among others.

The Ten Commandments in Exodus were for the 12 tribes in the desert, and the Ten Commandments in Deuteronomy were for the 12 tribes in the Promised Land with all the laws associated with the Temple, sacrifices, ablutions, national and land laws, etc. The last books written, Proverbs and the Writings, were specifically for the 12 tribes disbursed after their captivities in Assyria and Babylon and, beyond that, for ALL people.

Notice Solomon's prayer: "I am but a little child: I know not how to go out or come in" (1 Kings 3:7). Compare that with Proverbs 1:8: "My son, hear the instruction of your father, and forsake not the law of your mother." Solomon received his wisdom from His Father as a child; now, as a father, he's transmitting this wisdom to his children.

Solomon's Children, ALL people

Solomon had children, but the audience to whom he addresses Proverbs goes far beyond his own begotten family, his tribes, and even his nation. **Proverbs are for ALL people**; meditate on these passages.

6. *https://theexplanation.com/divine-design-god-formed-man-mental-health/*

Proverbs 1:4

Whoso is simple (Sam: ALL people), let him turn in here: as for **him** that wants understanding, *she* [wisdom] says to him.

Pro. 8:1 Does not wisdom cry? and understanding put forth her voice?

2 She stands in the **top of high places**, by the way in the **places of the paths.**

3 She cries at the **gates**, at the **entry of the city**, at the **coming in at the doors** (Sam: These Proverbs call out from EVERYWHERE to EVERYBODY).

4 **To you, O men**, I call; and my voice is to the **sons of man** (Sam: and daughters... ALL people).

Pro. 8:35 For **whoso** (Sam: anyone, anywhere) finds me finds *life* (Sam: mental health), and shall obtain favour of the LORD.

36 But **he** (Sam: everyone, everywhere) that sins against me *wrongs his own soul* (Sam: mental ILL-health): all they that hate me love death.

Pro. 9:3 She [wisdom] has sent forth her maidens: she cries upon the **highest places of the city**, (Sam: calls all in the city). **Whoso** is simple, let him turn in here:

The Book of Proverbs and all The Writings are not limited to Israelites or the Judeo-Christian Bible world. It is for ALL people worldwide who want mental health and to know how to deal with anxiety, depression, grief, race, God, justice, and many other daily aspects of life. These are the books of Bible Psychology.

10 Commandments in Proverbs for Everyone, Everywhere

The 10 Commandments are very much alive. The 10 Commandments are the wisdom of Proverbs calling from everywhere to everyone. Listen up. Here are the new Proverbs 10 Commandments:

Exodus – Deut.: 10 Commandments	Proverbs: 10 Commandments
1. You shall have no other gods before me	1:7 The fear of the LORD is the beginning of knowledge...
2. You shall make no idols	12:15 The way of a fool is right in his own eyes...
3. You shall not take God's name in vain	30:9 Lest I say... Who is the LORD? Or lest I... take the name of my God in vain.
4. Keep the Sabbath day holy	20:26 It is a snare to the man who devours that which is holy...
5. Honor your father and mother	6:21 My son, keep your father's commandments, and forsake not the law of your mother:
6. You shall not kill	6:16 Things the LORD hates: …hands that shed innocent blood
7. You shall not commit adultery	6:32 But whoso commits adultery with a woman lacks understanding: he that does it destroys his own soul.
8. You shall not steal	9:17-18 Stolen waters are sweet... But he knows not that the dead are there; and that her guests are in the depths of hell.
9. Do not bear false witness	6:19 The LORD hates: A false witness that speaks lies, and he that sows discord among brethren.
10. You shall not covet	21:26 The desire of the slothful kills him. He covets greedily all the day long:

Figure 8. Ten Commandments in Exodus and Proverbs

God gave and continually shouts the 10 Commandments from the pages of the Bible. Will we listen and benefit from mental health or remain deaf fools and harvest mental ill-health?

Many Books about Psychology

Notice God's Response to Solomon's request for wisdom: "... none like you before you, **neither after you**." God gave him understanding (Biblical Hebrew meaning, among others, *publish*). Solomon, through the Bible, *publishes* the wisdom to reach mental health. And God's Promise is: Nobody after him would improve on this wisdom!

That's why Solomon ended his book Ecclesiastes this way.

> **Ecclesiastes 12:12-14**
>
> 12 And further, by these, my son, be admonished: of making **many *books* there is no end**; and **much *study* is a weariness** of the flesh.
>
> 13 Let us hear the conclusion of the whole matter: Fear God, and keep his ***commandments***: for this is the whole duty of man.
>
> 14 For God shall bring every work into judgment, with every secret thing, whether it be good, or whether it be evil.

Psychology today spends billions studying the brain to determine what consciousness and mind are and how they work. Yes, they found a few things, but psychology is empty-headed. It looks to books by Sigmund Freud, Carl Jung, and Jordan Peterson; the list of psychologists and their books is endless[7]. I'm not saying there isn't value in such thinkers

7. https://en.wikipedia.org/wiki/List_of_psychologists

and books. I am saying they don't hold a candle to the wisdom of Solomon and the Writings on how to nurture and heal mental health.

It's time for practical applied psychology from Proverbs, starting with keeping God's 10 Commandments, the whole duty of humans, to nurture and heal minds.

22. Proverbs: Humanity's Guidebook

Proverbs is not just a book; it's a comprehensive sacred reference text for humanity, offering instructions on every aspect of life.

Solomon asks God for instructions to *govern* His people in his selfless prayer.

> 1 Kings 3:9
>
> Give therefore your servant an understanding heart to judge your people, that I may discern between good and bad.

God more than answered his prayer by making Solomon the wisest leader of all times, bar Christ, of Whom the righteous Solomon was a precursor. Nobody has published more pertinent books on life and leadership guidelines. He is the secular life coach par excellence, and Proverbs is the prime example of these instructions for everyone.

Proverbs are Rules for Life

Proverbs 1:11

> The *proverbs* (H4912) of Solomon the son of David, king of Israel;

We may consider the word *proverb* a quaint inspirational maxim, but it is much more in Biblical Hebrew.

H4912

> מָשָׁל mâshâl maw-shawl'; apparently from H4910 (מָשַׁל) in some original sense of superiority in mental action; properly, a pithy maxim, usually of metaphorical nature; hence, a simile (as an adage, poem, discourse):

> KJV - byword, like, parable, proverb.

H4910

> מָשַׁל mâshal maw-shal'; a primitive root; to rule:

> KJV - (have, make to have) dominion, governor, × indeed, reign, (bear, cause to, have) rule(-ing, -r), have power.

Mashal in modern Hebrew is the root of the word *government* (memshala). As an interesting side note, although I'm unsure of its grammatical value, the three letters of *mashal* (משל) and *shalom* (שלם) are identical. Also, consider that in Hebrew, Solomon is *Shlomo* (שְׁלֹמֹה), a derivative of shalom. If we put the story together, Proverbs are instructions for peace given by Peace—*Mashal* by *Shlomo*. Meditate on the depth of shalom, which you can study here[1]. That is peace of mind and mental health.

1. https://theexplanation.com/shalom-common-hebrew-greeting-no-idea-meaning/

Remember WHY God gave humans neshama and ruach, consciousness, and mind. We are to be Kings and Priests[2], that is, Rulers. These *mashalim*, proverbs, are rules, instructions about how to rule ourselves and others. This manual prepares us for our lives now and in the future.

Figure 9. Eccl. 12:13 Whole man keeps the Commandments

In the last Chapter, I quoted Ecclesiastes 12:13: "Let us hear the conclusion of the whole matter: Fear God, and keep his commandments: for this is the whole duty of man." In Hebrew, the verse is more explicit; [*duty*] was added to the translation. Check it at UnlockBibleMeaning.com via the Interlinear Bible[3]. It reads, "Fear God, and keep his commandments: for this is *the whole man*." At the beginning of this verse, there are two injunctions: *Fear God* and *keep*

2. https://theexplanation.com/gods-goal-humans-caring-for-humans-earth-why/

3. https://UnlockBibleMeaning.com

his commandments. Fear God summarizes the first four of the Ten Commandments, while *Keep His Commandments* is a resume of the last six.

To be a *whole man* and *woman*, keep the Ten Commandments and let the instructions of Proverbs be your guide. That's the way to whole health, including peace of mind; this is the way to beat anxiety; it's true holistic healing.

The Commandments and Proverbs are Guardrails

Unfortunately, we hear about people falling because they didn't use the guardrail. Or hikers on unprotected paths with sheer cliffs. We are all subject to the hazards of life and need solid guardrails and instructions to keep us on the right track. Our inner defects and outer influences continually affect our mental stability. Hence, we need a pillar to steady us and keep us upright and heading in the right direction.

That's the role of the Commandments and instructions in Proverbs.

Figure 10. Commandments and Proverbs are guardrails

Mind Refreshed is the book of Bible psychology instructions leading your consciousness and mind to mental health; this has nothing to do with religion, doctrine, Church, beliefs, or practices. You are a God-created human; He knows exactly how you function and sent along the Manual with all the necessary instructions. Like humans, a product cannot and does not know how to repair and maintain itself. In the diagram, the 10 Commandments and Proverbs are the guardrails that channel our internal and external influences, keeping them on the pathway of mental health.

Psalm 139:13-14

> 13 For you [God] have possessed my reins: You have covered me in my mother's womb.
>
> 14 I will praise you; for I am fearfully and wonderfully made: Marvellous are your works; And that my soul knows right well.

King David knew, without a doubt, that God was his Maker, as He is ours. Our bodies and minds are unique; we must take care of them. Some look at rules as constraints and outside control. No, everything has rules for proper usage. The real question is, will I CHOOSE my Maker's Rules and apply self-discipline and self-restraint? Or will I follow my own imagination, studies, and conceptions about mental health?

A Practical Workbook

The first part of this book resolved both the existence and nature of consciousness and mind. We must know what we're dealing with before we can nurture and heal. The WHY and HOW are solved; now we move on to WHAT we can and must do for the optimum operation of these two spirits we possess. WHAT we are to do to make them work in harmony, and the instructions to apply to bring mental health. Hence, there is a need for a workbook with practical exercises.

Here's an image revealing our mental makeup's major and offspring areas. It outlines the five areas of consciousness and their derivatives; the activities where the mind operates. We could graft many other characteristics onto these branches. These traits sum up the entire human being and society and the relationship between both.

Five Traits of Consciousness and Mind with Details				
Reasoning	**Purpose**	**Conduct**	**Socialization**	**Rulership**
Observation, Intuition	Space-time	Two-faced	Human Society	Human Government
Philosophy	Creativity	Free Will	Unique Individual	Governance Structure
Science	Imagination	Behavior	Gender Equality	Gov't for the People
Religion	Learning	Ethics	Bride & Groom	Human Needs
Theology	Choices	Justice	Couple Relationship	Inner Peace
	Growth Mindset	Self-reproach	Marriage	Peace of Mind
	Facing Challenges	Forgiveness	Family	National, Individual Prosperity
	Rule Life		Parenting	Individual vs. Collective Rights
	Responsible		Extended Family	Gov't Organization
			Ethnicity	Best Form of Gov't
			Nations	
			Language	
			Globalization	

Figure 11. Details of the five traits of consciousness

These values cover every aspect of individual and collective human society. Each of us is a customized mixture of all these traits to one degree or another. To a large extent, corporate bodies like companies, associations, clubs, etc., are characterized by a majority of these characteristics and play an essential role in the fabric of society.

The positive or negative scope, or amalgamation of all these markers, denotes our mental state, healthy or not. Insofar as these personal qualities, assailed by our internal and society's external influences, are within the guardrails of the *good* of the Tree of Good and Evil[4], we benefit from mental health. On the other hand, if our inner fears and outer forces overpower us, we sink into mental ill-health

Healing Mental Health

> Healing mental health means favorably leveraging our thoughts and actions concerning those inner fears and outer forces.

4. https://theexplanation.com/proverbs-10-commandments-humankind-21st-century/

God gave us the Proverbs guidelines to identify our thoughts and actions and show us their positive and negative results.

Proverbs are prods to jump-start our mental journey and accelerate the mental health healing process.

The key is that each of the approximately 800 proverb instructions can be associated with one or more mental traits and actions in the above diagram.

Each of us is different; no detailed instructions fit all. This workbook contains ten exercises (a 10-week program) for general consumption, but even there, I'll show you how to personalize them.

We increasingly see players on sports teams arguing with the referee over the application of rules. Unfortunately, a similar approach can affect us when studying or meditating on God's Word. Rules in sports and the Bible are not there because the referee or God wants to control us, to the contrary. Those guidelines are there so the game runs smoothly despite two opposing teams or, in our case, two opposing pulls, one to the *good*, the other to the *evil*. It's always our choice. Warring Proverbs[5], as I call them, reveal this pull between good and evil and encourage us toward the good.

Focus on a Proverb/Action for a Week

The goal is to determine what specific aspect, and I do mean precise detail, of your character you will focus your attention on this week. Which of the five areas of consciousness do you need to work on (ex. Purpose)? Within that area, what precise characteristic needs explicit attention (ex. Learning

5. https://theexplanation.com/warring-proverbs-each-fighting-the-good-fight/

more about such and such, depending on your specific Purpose)?

Find a Proverb that explicitly addresses your phobia, twisted view, thought, purpose, or habit that's causing you hardship, and that's your daily action exercise for the week; this is what you want to write out, keep with you, pray about, meditate on, study, and talk to others about ways and methods to apply this Proverb, this rule. Brainstorm, journal your ideas, and especially PRACTICE them; this is not theoretical, it is PRACTICAL. Faith without works is dead. Brainstorming with action is also dead.

Do this for a week because *six days shall you work, and the seventh day is the day of* ***rest***, meaning *ceasing* and *refreshing* your thinking process. To meditate on your last week's backsliding or hopefully progress, and establish a plan for the next week. Adam and Eve had the Sabbath, the 7th Day with God, immediately after their 6th Day Creation. They, like God, didn't need physical rest; they needed mental stimulation to prepare them for the upcoming week. Unfortunately for them it became a *down* week.

We should evaluate our action plan in relation to our chosen Proverb and see our balance of good and evil. Positive growth means better mental health. Little by little, week by week, we improve.

Look at this practical exercise and use it as a template[6] for your own Proverbs Bible study and personal mental health program.

We will give more advice in the practical exercises. But if you don't feel up to it, you might need or already have a Bible-oriented psychologist. It's time to talk and share this with them.

---

6. https://theexplanation.com/practical-mind-transformation-first-steps/

- Find or speak with your mentor, family, or other caregiver.
- Find practical situations where you can apply the Proverb.
- Adapt the instructions for age, frame of mind, or difficulty.
- Set up your daily and weekly plans.
- Discuss them and their results with people you're at ease with and who can give you constructive advice.
- Move to the next little step.
- Keep moving, even if you go sideways or backward occasionally.

I'd love to hear about your experience as an inspiration for all of us to improve our mental health.

23. Mental Health: 1000 Therapy Picks

Try choosing among the over 1000 alternative therapies and treatments for mental illnesses, not to mention the therapists and their adaptations. Worst, dangerous, best. Nightmare.

Just as there is confusion in defining consciousness and mind[1], so there is with alternative therapies when something goes wrong. Unfortunately, it's normal. If you took your car to a garage for repair and the mechanic told you, "I've never seen that before and don't know what it is, but leave it with me, and I'll fix it." Would you be inclined to have confidence? I doubt it.

> **NB** I am not a psychologist. This book gives a Biblical perspective on consciousness and mind, the why, how, and what. This book focuses on general mild psychological

1. https://www.researchgate.net/publication/377744305_A_landscape_of_consciousness_Toward_a_taxonomy_of_explanations_and_implications

issues. We all live with phobias and, to some degree, are twisted by our internal and external influences. Most handle it well, but anxiety, stress, and depression are significant issues today. This book can help.

Alternative Therapies to be Very Careful With, Better to Avoid

There are severe mental disorders that affect the subconscious, where there's a disconnection from reality. First, we should avoid all practices that would put us in such a state. Psychedelic drugs and practices like Kundalini yoga or cleansing are not a way to meet God; they are precisely the opposite. Hypnosis and practices where you lose control of your mind can be dangerous. Out-of-body experiences, voices in your head, and Ouija boards, despite their reputation, will lead you away from Divine Direction.

We should abstain from Eastern philosophic practices, including meditation[2], mindfulness[3], visualization, manifesting[4], mind cleansing, or other activities that focus the mind on repetitive, rhythmic sounds, words, mantras, and music to explore our souls. They come short in at least two areas.

Meditation

Bible meditation, including Proverbs, is the best and only meditation you should engage in.

2. https://www.npr.org/sections/health-shots/2024/03/31/1241784635/meditation-vipassana-dangerous-mental-health
3. https://theconversation.com/meditation-can-be-harmful-and-can-even-make-mental-health-problems-worse-230435
4. https://www.psychologytoday.com/us/basics/manifesting

The book of Psalms outlines Bible meditation; King David gives us the perfect example. Search for *meditate* at UnlockBibleMeaning.com[5]. We are to meditate on physical and spiritual realities: the works of God's Hands, His Creation, Law, Precepts, Statutes, and God's Word. When we understand God's Plan for us and humanity, what the tumultuous present portends, how to balance faith in God and the confusion of this world, and what God has prepared for us and all of humanity, it all lends to mental health. It beats all alternative therapies, hands down.

Human Conduct

Most alternative therapies tell you wisdom is already within you; you simply need to access it. These methods do precisely what the Serpent told Eve, "...your eyes shall be opened, and you shall be as gods knowing good and evil" (Genesis 3:5). You can know and make the rules. No.

Let's put the cards on the table; humans alone cannot know Divine Spirituality. God Himself says, "The heart is deceitful above all things, and desperately wicked: who can know it?" (Jeremiah 17:9). Only with God's Wisdom can we know the heart. That's the first step in Conduct, realizing we're two-faced. We should avoid any alternative therapy that side-steps this fundamental Biblical knowledge.

Demons

Biblically, demons are genuine and not to be invoked or sought out. This book does not broach these dangerous subjects, which require experienced handlers. It also does not touch on Biblical Spirituality and the Holy Spirit. Please see *Mind-Body Problem Solved*[6] for the harmful effects of wrong mind practices and the correct form of Biblical Spirituality.

---

5. https://unlockbiblemeaning.com

6. *https://TheExplanation.com/mind*

The Foundation for Mental Health Therapy

Nobody knows what consciousness and mind are, and yet we blindly have faith in therapists who treat our most precious commodity. Unfortunately, without that basic knowledge, it's no wonder that alternative therapies are plethoric. Everyone can imagine a solution to fix your mind, and many do. Here's a list of alternative therapie[7]s and cognitive behavioral therapies[8]. I'm not trying to confuse you, but you must realize that the most critical human domain is in tohu va bohu - darkness and turmoil.

I could evaluate each of the alternative therapies and rate them from 1 to 10, but I don't want to waste my or your time. Let's proceed another way. *The Explanation* will give you the criteria to identify the proper psychotherapy you need. This book has already pinpointed those values. Here they are once again.

The key to consider is that all the values in the diagram below must be based on the Bible. God created and infused consciousness and mind, neshama and ruach, in each of us. He knows how they work, and He gave us His Word in which He gives us those instructions.

Five Traits of Consciousness and Mind with Details				
Reasoning	**Purpose**	**Conduct**	**Socialization**	**Rulership**
Observation, Intuition	Space-time	Two-faced	Human Society	Human Government
Philosophy	Creativity	Free Will	Unique Individual	Governance Structure
Science	Imagination	Behavior	Gender Equality	Gov't for the People
Religion	Learning	Ethics	Bride & Groom	Human Needs
Theology	Choices	Justice	Couple Relationship	Inner Peace
	Growth Mindset	Self-reproach	Marriage	Peace of Mind
	Facing Challenges	Forgiveness	Family	National, Individual Prosperity
	Rule Life		Parenting	Individual vs. Collective Rights
	Responsible		Extended Family	Gov't Organization
			Ethnicity	Best Form of Gov't
			Nations	
			Language	
			Globalization	

7. https://en.wikipedia.org/wiki/List_of_psychotherapies

8. https://en.wikipedia.org/wiki/List_of_cognitive%E2%80%93behavioral_therapies

Figure 12. Five traits of consciousness & mind, details

Which alternative therapy is closest to these values?

1. Teaches finding a Proverb or Bible verse (this is Bible Talk Therapy).
2. Upgrades your life (improving your conduct and thought processes).
3. Transforms your mind and actions (the reality of daily life).
4. Coincides with Biblical instruction (God's Word is the foundation of all knowledge).

The psychological therapy that comes closest to applying these criteria is the best. Beware of alternative therapies that deviate from these guidelines; the more, the worse they are.

Cognitive Behavior Therapy

I'm hesitating whether to refer to CBT here. That's Cognitive Behavioral Therapy. Here's what Wikipedia says[9]:

> CBT is a common form of talk therapy based on the combination of the basic principles from ***behavioral*** and ***cognitive*** psychology.
>
> CBT is a "problem-focused" and "action-oriented" form of therapy, meaning it is used to treat specific problems related to a diagnosed mental disorder. The therapist's role is to assist the client in finding and practicing effective strategies to address the identified goals and to alleviate symptoms of the disorder.

9. https://en.wikipedia.org/wiki/Cognitive_behavioral_therapy

> CBT is based on the belief that thought distortions and maladaptive behaviors play a role in the development and maintenance of many psychological disorders and that symptoms and associated distress can be reduced by teaching new information-processing skills and coping mechanisms.

This statement has pros and cons, starting with the name Cognitive Behavioral Therapy:

1. In traditional psychology, ***cognitive*** refers to the scientific study of mental processes.[10] We've seen that confusion. In the above diagram, consciousness (neshama Genesis 2:7) and mind (ruach Job 32:8, the *spirit in man*) are the title, the overseeing originators of the five aspects of humanity conferred on humans by God: That is Biblical *cognitive.*
2. In psychology circles, ***behavioral*** refers to a systematic approach to understanding the behavior of humans and other animals[11]. Again, there's confusion about how humans should behave, and since we're not descendants of animals, they shouldn't be considered. In the above diagram, we have *Conduct* with the seven major phases of behavior according to God's Word. Taken together, that is Biblical *behavior.*

Assembling the two concepts of *Cognitive Behavior* in pertinent Bible terms, it is more appropriate to refer to *Mental Conduct. Mental* includes neshama and ruach, while *Conduct* is the gamut of how humans function, including the thinking and action processes. Animals act, but they do not think per se. Humans need a nurturing and healing method for *Mental Conduct.*

---

10. https://en.wikipedia.org/wiki/Cognitive_psychology

11. https://en.wikipedia.org/wiki/Behaviorism

Bible Proverbs Method

Note that we're not using the term Christian psychology because this method is not limited to Christians; it's for everyone worldwide. We must base psychology on Biblical understanding:

1. *Mental (Cognitive)* is neshama and ruach, possessed by everyone.
2. *Conduct (Behavior)* involves good and evil, with ethics (rules) to follow. Disobedience brings justice, leading to self-reproach, rehabilitation, and forgiveness. This behavioral pathway is valid for everyone.

These two criteria (mental and conduct) should be the standard measure for all mental health alternative therapies. I know that most caregivers propose mental health services because they innately feel they're helpful, and many do have certain benefits. But the further mental health alternative therapies are from this foundation, the more dangerous they become.

The Explanation thinks the *Bible Proverbs Method* is a good name for the proposed process.

> 1. The ***Bible*** is where we must go to define *mental/cognition,* the action of acquiring knowledge. That's why we had to start this book with the Biblical origin of neshama and ruach and explain why only humans possess the former. I realize I did not explain the chasmic difference of ruach in animals and humans. Please see *Mind-Body Problem Solved*[12]. The essential is that ruach in animals[13] allows them to accomplish their particular species' one-and-only way of life.

---

12. *https://TheExplanation.com/body*

13. https://theexplanation.com/the-role-of-the-ruach-spirit-in-living-beings/

A dog will always have a dog life. A buffalo will always have a buffalo life. But human life is a person's choice; no two lives are identical. With humans, ruach activates our personality[14], character, skills, and choices. We are one in eight billion. The Bible alone explains this, hence the *Bible Proverbs Method.*

2. *Proverbs* is where we must find the ***behavior*** within the ***conduct*** that characterizes all human beings. Behavior is the third of the seven phases of human conduct: Two-faced, free will, behavior, ethics, justice, self-reproach, and forgiveness. Those foundational elements of conduct must be dealt with equitably to produce mental health. Alternative therapies may recommend some of them, all the better, but none practice all of them. They are incomplete.

3. *Method*, not *therapy*, because the latter is only for healing. We must include nurturing to minimize and even avoid healing.

In the last chapter[15], *The Explanation* detailed the ***Bible Proverbs Method*** in action exercises to develop and heal mental health. This book will end with ten practical exercises and instructions to personalize them and create new ones specifically for your mental health.

Today, many Judeo-Christian organizations, caregivers, and life coaches integrate Eastern philosophical concepts and practices for their congregations, patients, and members; I'm not saying there are no benefits. However, these are not divine procedures. *Bible Proverbs Method* is a Biblical practice that will help all with mental health.

---

14. https://theexplanation.com/ruach-in-the-bible-creates-human-superiority/

15. https://theexplanation.com/need-instructions-proverbs-humanitys-guidebook/

24. Nurture and Heal for Mental Health

Nurturing and healing are the combined solutions to achieve and preserve mental health in today's crisis.

We accentuate physical health to the detriment of mental health; we need both to nurture and heal the body and mind. The lack of nurturing in mental health is a significant cause of our mental illness crisis in your nation and worldwide. For a baby, mother's milk is the best physical food; what is the best mental food?

Nurture, The Foundation of Mental Health

Why is the nurture in *nurture and heal* so important, even more so than heal, even if we emphasize the latter? Nurturing is where everything starts. When we take nurturing seriously, we diminish healing by truckloads. Here's the definition of *nurture* from the Cambridge Dictionary[1].

1. https://dictionary.cambridge.org/us/dictionary/english/nurture

> To take care of, feed, and protect someone or something, especially young children or plants, and help him, her, or it to develop:

Nurturing mental health during the early years of a child's life is crucial, as it lays the foundation for emotional, psychological, and social well-being throughout life. The first few years of childhood are a critical period of mental and cognitive development, during which a child's environment, relationships, and experiences significantly influence their future mental health, cognitive abilities, and behavior.

Early childhood mental health refers to the child's ability to experience and regulate emotions, form close relationships, and explore their environment in ways that promote learning and development. Fostering good mental health during this period can help prevent mental troubles later in life and enhance a child's overall development.

Experiences during early childhood—positive or negative—are instrumental in forming mental pathways that affect behavior, learning, and emotional regulation. Nurturing leads to the proper development of consciousness and mind. The initial teaching of a child should be to know and reason between good and bad, have a purpose (like keeping their room tidy), conduct (obeying Dad and Mom), socialize with family and friends, and rule, self-control of their emotions and behavior, whether alone or with friends.

Positive experiences, such as loving care, consistent emotional support, and cognitive stimulation, contribute to healthy mental development, leading to resilience, social skills, and emotional regulation. Conversely, adverse experiences, such as neglect, abuse, or chronic stress, can disrupt normal mental health, potentially leading to issues such as anxiety, depression, or behavioral problems later in life.

While short-term stress can help children learn how to cope with challenges, chronic or toxic stress—such as exposure to violence, severe neglect, or family dysfunction—can have detrimental effects on one's mental perspective. Prolonged exposure to toxic stress can interfere with the development of critical areas of the mind, like decision-making, self-control, and processing emotions; this can lead to difficulties in managing feelings, forming healthy relationships, and handling stress as children grow older.

Nurturing mental health during the early years benefits the child and has broader societal implications. Children who develop stable emotional regulation, social competence, and resilience are likelier to grow into healthy, productive adults who contribute positively to society.

Parental Responsibility in Nurture and Heal

Parents, caregivers, educators, and communities all play a role in fostering healthy mental development, ensuring that children grow into emotionally healthy and capable adults who contribute positively to society. Supporting early childhood mental health extends beyond individual benefits, with ripple effects that touch families, communities, and the economy.

The family environment plays a crucial role in shaping an individual's mental health, especially during childhood and adolescence. While it may not be the only factor influencing mental well-being, the family is one of the most essential foundations for emotional and psychological development. Parents, siblings, and extended family members create a nurturing or harmful atmosphere that impacts mental health in profound ways. Understanding the roles of fathers, mothers, and siblings, coupled with strategies to foster mental health stability in future generations, is critical for ensuring long-term mental well-being.

In these troubled times, social roles and responsibilities are taking a beating. Somewhere, somehow, someone or an organization needs to take on the role of helping girls and boys, young women and men, learn their God-given role in society. We seem to have all sorts of professional courses to earn money, but what about how to live as individuals, families, and as a society, according to the Book of Proverbs? Babies, young children, and adolescents are not the problem; their caregivers, namely their progenitors, are. With 50% divorce rates, domestic violence, and abandonment, mental illness is, unfortunately, a given. We must turn this situation around to win the battle of nurture and healing.

The Major Problem with Nurturing

Individually and collectively, if we want our family and nation to return to normality, the best hope is to work with the next generation, our children; this presupposes a shockwave of awakening from parents and caregivers who are responsible for the next generation. On the other hand, the way to destroy families and the nation is to upheave parental responsibility. Here's a Bible example of Balaam, a prophet of God. Read the full story in Numbers 22-24 at UnlockBibleMeaning.com[2]. He was a prophet who got too close to the enemy for monetary gain. God stopped him from prophesying against Israel, so Balaam found another way to bring the nation to its ruin.

> **Revelation 2:14**
>
> But I have a few things against you, because you have there them that hold the doctrine of Balaam, who taught Balac to cast a *stumblingblock* (G4625) before the children of Israel, to eat things sacrificed to idols, and to commit fornication.

2. https://UnlockBibleMeaning.com

Balaam threw a wrench in the works. Look at the Greek meaning. There are a lot of these stumbling blocks going on today; think about fornication.

G4625

σκάνδαλον skandalon skan'-dal-on; A **scandal**; probably from a derivative of G2578; a trap stick (bent sapling) that is snare (figuratively cause of displeasure or sin):

KJV - occasion to fall, (of stumbling) offence, thing that offends, stumbling-block.

G2578

κάμπτω kamptō kamp'-to; Apparently a primary verb; to **bend:**

KJV - bow.

The concepts of *scandal* and *bend* refer to something that exists on a spectrum or a gradual sequence of increasingly *bending* the rules, leading to *scandals* without clear-cut boundaries between different points. When applying this to the long-term effects of being exposed to violent aggression, sexualized video games, movies, videos, strained gender relationships, dark media content, and certain rock and rap music, be it the tempo or lyrics, this affects mental health. Things get increasingly *bent* out of shape, more and more *fake,* with influencers and stars trying to outdo each other, vying for our attention; the environment in which we swim can slowly drown the weaker swimmers.

In Balaam's narrative, Israel collapsed. Will we follow the same poor example? The result is evident if we continue to nurture and heal negatively as we're doing.

Healing in Nurture and Heal

King David was subject to mood swings. Here's a well-known prayer to which I'd like to draw your attention. There are fundamental principles that need to be put in place to accelerate access to mental health.

> **Psalm 23:1-3**
>
> 1 [A Psalm of David.] The LORD is my shepherd; I shall not want.
>
> 2 He makes me to lie down in green pastures: he leads me beside the still waters.
>
> 3 He *restores* (H7725) my soul: he leads me in the paths of righteousness for his name's sake.

The way to *restore* mental health is to follow the path of righteousness. Note that *restore* means to return; the idea is to return to norms that align with Proverbs' righteousness.

> **H7725**
>
> שׁוּב shûwb shoob; a primitive root; to turn back (hence, away) transitively or intransitively, literally or figuratively (not necessarily with the idea of return to the starting point); generally to retreat; often adverbial, again:
>
> KJV - Sam: there are over 80 translations; here are the highlights: feed, rejoice, bring (back, home again), call (to mind), cease, convert, get (oneself) (back) again, go (back,

home), recover, refresh, relieve, rescue, restore, retrieve, reverse, make to turn self again,

In the context of the *Bible Proverbs Method*[3], David's plea to *restore my soul* means striving to align one's life with the Proverb principles in the areas of your life's Reasoning, Purpose, Conduct, Socialization, and Rulership. The ten practical lessons to apply that follow will show you how to *restore yourself.*

Notice where God leads David and all of us who desire to enable and accomplish this *recovery, returning home* to a saner frame of mind: *green pastures* and *still waters*. There's nothing like being in nature to hasten the restoration of mental health. But this is also figurative and refers to the appropriate environment for healing, animated by rational reasoning, a motivating purpose, an atmosphere conducive to correct conduct, supporting relationships, and the ability to learn to run your life responsibly.

Only within the framework of nurturing and healing, both in accord with Proverbs' wisdom, will we establish family and national settings and uplifting conditions to develop and rehabilitate lucid mental health.

---

3. *https://theexplanation.com/alternative-therapies-mental-health-worst-best/*

V. Exercises to Start Beating Anxiety

Part V is precisely WHAT each of us can do to improve our mental health and that of those people around us.

Request for a Book Review

I want to express my gratitude for reading *Mind Refreshed*. An honest review would mean a lot to me, and I would greatly appreciate it if you would use these questions for a review. Easy access is available via the review links[4] and QR code. (Info after the indexes)

- What did you like the most about what you've read?
- What two things have you learned that will help you?
- Does the author have the proper credentials?
- Did the book live up to its description or stated goal?

4. https://theexplanation.com/review-mr

25. Bible Proverbs Method: Sure Relief

What is the best therapy for anxiety? It's not a magic pill or method that remedies the discomfort instantly. *Bible Proverbs Method* for anxiety will work.

Anxiety Definition

It's time for practical lessons in therapy for anxiety. Let's see the overall process we will follow and why. Anxiety is distress of the mind. Here's a definition from the Cambridge Dictionary[1].

> An uncomfortable feeling of nervousness or worry about something that is happening or might happen in the future:

We've already established what the mind is[2] and that it is the activator of consciousness[3]; they work together in five areas[4]: reasoning, purpose,

---

1. https://dictionary.cambridge.org/dictionary/english/anxiety
2. https://theexplanation.com/bible-ruach-decoded-psychology-mental-activity/
3. https://theexplanation.com/2-spirits-neshama-ruach-reveal-human-essence/

conduct, socialization, and rulership. Since we understand consciousness and mind and how they work, we can now reveal how they best function optimally.

The human constitution has its fivefold base working harmoniously within the individual (internal influences[5]) and their position in society (external influences[6]).

> Anxiety occurs when one or more of these five traits: Reasoning, Purpose, Conduct, Socialization, and Rulership are out of balance.

The Therapy for Anxiety

To nurture, we must help our children align the five aspects of their consciousness. To heal, we must help anxiety-prone people REalign these five traits.

The baseline code to which we align, realign, or conform ourselves is the book of Proverbs—the universal code of life for all human beings today.

> **Proverbs 9:20, 22**
>
> 20 My son, attend to **my words**; incline your ear to my sayings.
>
> 22 For they are **life** to those that find them, and **health** to all their flesh (Sam: and mind).

The therapy for anxiety to reach **life** and **mental health** is simple: align yourself with **God's Words**, specifically those of Proverbs. Remember,

4. https://theexplanation.com/unraveling-purpose-inside-scoop-unique-humans/

5. https://theexplanation.com/powerful-influences-mental-health-starts-womb/

6. https://theexplanation.com/powerful-influences-mental-health-starts-womb/

this has nothing to do with religion, church, or even spirituality; this is the recipe for an anxiety-free life, or at least for reducing stress.

Please don't get me wrong. This lifestyle doesn't mean you won't have any problems or angst. It means you'll be able to work through the mishaps and troubles because your focus aligns with the book of Proverbs. Your ear will be inclined to God's Sayings, and there are Godly Maxims and Principles about every aspect of life that will help us pull through and see it from God's anti-anxious, not our anxious-prone point of view.

Therapy for Anxiety - 1st Lesson: Reasoning Skills Prove a Higher Power

Sixty years ago, I hadn't used my reasoning skills to determine whether a Higher Power exists. I have now. What about you?

Let's take a slightly different tack on this question. Is there Something above us? Something bigger than humans, more prominent than our minds, our intelligence? It doesn't matter what you want to call It; that's not the point.

I'm not trying to trick or mislead you. But I would like you to use your reasoning skills. Reasoning is the first aspect of consciousness[7], as I've defined in this book *Mind Refreshed*. Of course, I've talked about God because I'm no longer agnostic. But this isn't about me; it's about you, the readers. How did humans alone acquire the capacity to reason? Activate your reasoning skills to figure that one out.

This is the first practical exercise for the *Bible Proverbs Method*. For one week, we will focus on one specific area of consciousness (reasoning) and drill down to one precise point: Is there a Higher Power? I hear

7. https://theexplanation.com/mystery-of-human-conduct-origin-wonders-woes/

you. Yes, that's a huge, *precise point*. Why this focus? Here's our Proverb for the week.

Proverbs 1:7

The fear of the LORD is the beginning of knowledge: but fools despise wisdom and instruction.

Reasoning skills are based on correct knowledge; we'd all agree on that. They are the very foundation; the beginning of this process is the *fear of the Lord*. If you don't know IF there's a Higher Power, your reasoning skills are on shaky ground, not to say quicksand. This verse tells us the Lord's reasoning skills are way more advanced than ours; if we want true wisdom and instruction (who doesn't?), then we'd do well to approve (the opposite of *despise*) the Lord's reasoning skills are above our own.

So, can we prove (I chose that word carefully) that there is a Higher Power? Let the Bible answer.

Romans 1:19-20

19 Because that which may be known of God is manifest in them [humans]; for God has shewed it to them.

20 For the invisible things of him from the creation of the world are clearly seen, being understood by the *things that are made*, even his eternal power and Godhead; so that they are without excuse:

This passage states the *invisible things,* science would say immaterial or intangible, of him, this Higher Power, are clearly seen, meaning we can prove, beyond a shadow of a doubt, that His Eternal Power exists. Wow, that's powerful. How? *By the things that are made*, translated *workmanship* in Ephesians 2:10. The Higher Power's Workmanship, His Creation, is the inexcusable proof of His Existence and reasoning skills.

It's time to spend a week focusing your thinking on His Workmanship because reverence for Him is the beginning of understanding everything. Otherwise, we are both ignorant and *without excuse* before our Creator.

> A well-organized education should not be one which prepares students for good remuneration alone. It should be one that can help and guide them towards acquiring clear thinking, a fruitful mind, and an elevated spirit.
>
> –Haile Selassie

Exercise your Reasoning Skills

Which came first, the chicken or the egg? The dumbest question of all is really the most intelligent question, and it can test one's belief in a Higher Power. Here's the follow-up. How many generations would it take to evolve a chicken or an egg? Well, if you didn't already have both, you'd never even get a second generation!

Here's King David's practical wisdom as part of this week's exercise.

> **Psalm 143:5**
>
> I remember the days of old; I *meditate* (H1897) on all your *works* (H4639); I *muse* (H7878) on the work of your hands.

Bible meditation is not focusing on your breath, a word, or some incomprehensible mantra. Breathing exercises can help during panic attacks, but beyond that, along with other focusing exercises, they do not help transform your mind, which is the seat of worry and anxiety.

Bible meditation does because it leads you to understand there's a Higher Power Who can take care of you. This exercise is to learn of His Existence and begin to know Him.

See what this Bible *meditation* exercise is about. Check it at UnlockBibleMeaning.com[8].

H1897

הָגָה hâgâh daw-gaw'; a primitive root (compare H1901 (הָגִיג)); to murmur (in pleasure or anger); by implication, to ponder:

KJV - imagine, meditate, mourn, mutter, roar, × sore, speak, study, talk, utter.

H7878

שִׂיחַ sîyach see'-akh; a primitive root; to ponder, i.e. (by implication) converse (with oneself, and hence, aloud) or (transitively) utter:

KJV - commune, complain, declare, meditate, muse, pray, speak, talk (with).

Meditate on the Universe and the Human Body

We can develop proper reasoning skills through studying, praying, and speaking about God's Works; the *invisible* things of Him that are made from the creation of the world are clearly seen. Here's a video documentary about God's Creation aptly entitled *Invisible Universe*

8. https://UnlockBibleMeaning.com

Revealed[9]. Watch and meditate about the puniness of humans and the existence of a Higher Power.

At 35 minutes, the video touches on the expanding Universe and Dark Matter. Generally, something propelled into the sky will slow down and fall back to Earth. But we find the Universe's expansion speeding up, activated by a mysterious Dark Energy. Sure, we can say we don't know what it is, and it's easy to say that's proof of God. Maybe yes, maybe no. But we must realize these colossal forces exist, and science has no idea of their origin. That's the macro level, now the micro level.

> **Psalm 139:14**
>
> I will praise you [God]; for I am fearfully and wonderfully made: marvellous are your works; and that my soul knows right well.

As with King David, take the time to realize how fearfully and wonderfully you're made. Here are a few subjects to study:

Chronobiology[10]: The just-in-time arrival of two or more elements. In building DNA, our bodies generate nucleotides that arrive in the proper sequence at the exact moment to construct the DNA strand.

Apoptosis[11]**:** The process of cells dying at just the right moment, in the exact places where events occur. In forming fingers and toes, your limbs first form as paddles, and at about ten weeks of pregnancy, the cells between the future fingers and toes die.

Protein folding[12]: After forming long protein strands, each folds into a specific shape to form a motor that allows your body to function, like

9. *https://youtu.be/BjkNI96Dg-w*

10. https://theexplanation.com/pollination-chronobiology-flora-how-it-works/

11. https://theexplanation.com/apoptosis-programmed-cell-death-even-before-birth/

a pump that permits specific molecules only into a cell. This folding process is highly complex and takes place in seconds.

Critical thinking should help you realize that these three, out of thousands of bodily systems, at practically an invisible, micro level, are streamlined, unique, all-or-nothing, integrated, designed parts of our wonderfully made bodies, as King David said. It can't be any other way.

The Universe we exist in, the Earth we live on, the air we breathe, the water we drink, and the food we eat witness the Existence and Power of Something much higher than humans. Use your reasoning skills to see it because it is the beginning of knowledge leading to fuller mental health.

With Reasoning orientation, we can get immediate, measurable, and positive results, which is a tremendous encouragement. The *Bible Proverbs Method* for beating anxiety is underway.

---

12. https://theexplanation.com/protein-folding-machines-continual-movement-keep-body-running-smoothly/

26. Purpose. Hit Your Bullseye

When you step out of the house, you want to know where you're going. Likewise, establish goals in your life.

So, let's lay out this second lesson with exercises to focus on PURPOSE for one week. It's the second of the five traits of consciousness and the guiding light to the following three aspects: conduct, socialization, and rulership.

> **Proverbs 29:18**
>
> Where there is no *vision* (purpose), the people perish...

This world can be ugly; some people don't see a future or have lost hope in tomorrow. They will perish mentally; no future is a sure formula for anxiety.

You must have an overriding pursuit in your life. Something big, more vast, and better than you are at this moment that you can devote your mind, time, and energy to for 20, 30, or 50 years. In this context, let's talk about your professional life. That brings in the money; yes, you need that, and it aids with accomplishing all the other goals in your life.

Think about a ship leaving port and its purpose: Get passengers to their future dream destination.

1. It must know its END destination.
2. It must know how to get out of its present port. For this maneuver, its second-by-second surveillance often requires a local pilot and even tug-boats.

That is the same as the trip of life, the therapy for anxiety.

Destination and First Step

1. What is your FUTURE destination?
   Your PURPOSE: Train-driver, doctor, social worker, artist, pilot, entrepreneur...

That's a big destination decision where you'll navigate rough waters. You'll gain experience during the trip and make course changes to keep on track. You must know yourself, your capacities, and your mindset. You cannot do this alone, but you are ultimately responsible for reaching the proper ports of call and, finally, your destination.

You don't have to make FINAL destination choices at age 18, 20, or even 30, but you need an excellent idea of some intermediary ports, or you will be doing circles in shark-infested waters. Goals change; it's *flexible steadfastness*.

2. How are you maneuvering to get out of the harbor

TODAY? In the next hour? NOW?

Your PURPOSE today: What's today's ONE step forward toward becoming a train driver, doctor, social worker, artist, pilot, or entrepreneur...

With your COMPASS, you can modify a course, even one small degree, to align yourself in the right direction. As a parent, psychologist, teacher, manager, or coach, it's your responsibility to help point a child, patient, student, employee, or client in the right direction and show them HOW to take the FIRST step. Help them DEVELOP the **how-to,** step-by-step plan, and receive the TRAINING and EQUIPMENT (the intermediary ports) to launch their journey.

Cast off ONE of the ropes attached to the moorings, the first detaching of a shackle imprisoning you in the harbor. Jump the first, even lowest, hurdle in front of you. That's your initial victory to conquer anxiety.

Realize you did it. Help the person monitor their performance, even if you/they make a mistake. A cruise, like the therapy for anxiety, starts with one tiny maneuver. ONE stage at a time, the what and how you'll accomplish that. Don't overwhelm yourself or another person. Time is not the significant factor here; the person and their initial stride forward are.

A mistake in accomplishing the task is not a critical issue here; trying is; we all make mistakes. Analyze why the person tripped over the hurdle and how s/he/you can be helped to jump better. Maybe reduce the height. Perhaps you need to add a stage you hadn't thought of, like getting a more adapted pair of shoes or doing some leg-muscle building first if you're a passive person becoming more active.

It's why the therapy for anxiety focuses on one Proverb, one step for a week. Meditate, pray, study, and talk to family and friends about it. Read articles (Benefits of cooking on mental health[1]. Why eggs with a

1. https://www.news-medical.net/health/Mental-Health-and-Cooking.aspx

recipe?[2]), visit the library, and find a good book; summarize a few steps to follow. Think out of the box (quote: You don't have to see the whole staircase; just take the first step), vary the methods, try something new, and find related Proverbs, parables, and Bible examples; this is practical Bible meditation. On the seventh day, you can analyze your maneuver and map out the subsequent two or three actions needed to get out of port.

Personalize Your Therapy for Anxiety

Whether it's for yourself or if you're a coach, trainer, manager, employer, teacher, parent, adult, adolescent, or child, personalize each step of the therapy for anxiety for the concerned person.

- Consider their age, mental level, intellectual, and manual skills.
    - Mastery of space: cleanup; organize a drawer, cupboard, room, all the way up to a factory or office; it depends on the capacity and state of the individual.
- Consider establishing a detailed *how-to* to reach each benchmark
    - Learn a subject or skill, or enhance a talent you've always been intrigued by. Get one fact, move, and add more. Coaching might be necessary.
- Make each step short and attainable *quickly* so they can know they've crossed the finish line.
    - Let their physical or mental creativity begin to simmer. Help their **imagination** to flow. Just so long as it's legal and edifying. Compose stories, try drawing, pottery, and many other endeavors.

2. https://www.wellandgood.com/brain-benefits-eggs/

In discussing the stage with them, remember the seven steps of Conduct[3]. Maneuvers cannot be imposed. It must be their free will choice, just as with their behavior, whether to apply the step or not. There's self-reproach, recognition of one's error, and forgiveness of oneself from you and God. They're responsible for their decisions. They set the goal and are accountable.

This chart, the COMPASS, tracks the destination and the vision you're working toward. The goal is accurate, and the little-by-little steps in the five vital areas of consciousness will strike the target. The second week focuses on the vision and the purpose so we do not perish; to the contrary, anxiety is diminishing.

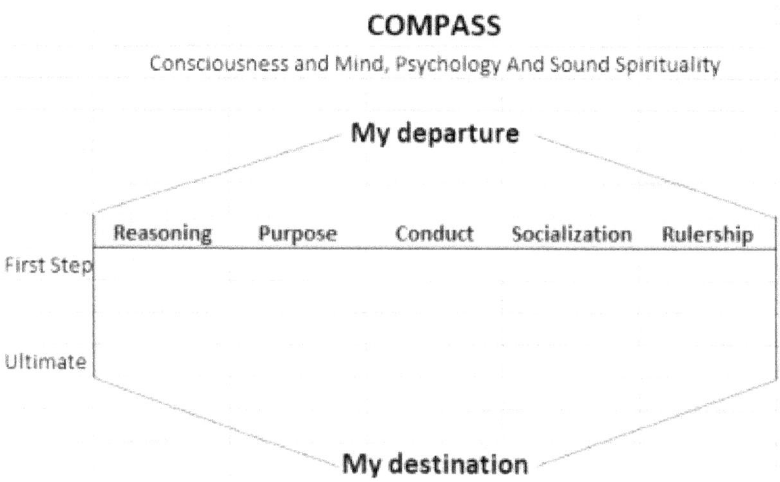

Figure 13. Compass to my sound mind destination

3. https://theexplanation.com/mystery-of-human-conduct-origin-wonders-woes/

Download (Google Doc)[4] and print a copy to plot and follow your cruise. You'll find more details and examples about COMPASS at this link[5], and you can leave comments and suggestions.

Example and Results of Therapy for Anxiety: Purpose

Many years ago, in London, I went into this food store with a grill behind the counter. A disabled young man was learning to fry eggs. His manager patiently showed him how to clean, prepare the grill, break the egg (no shells and no broken yolk), and use a spatula to position it on the plate. A few days later, I returned, and he was doing a perfect job. One by one, he'd mastered the cooking steps and was autonomous.

Fry an egg and break down all the steps. If you have a young child, watch, guide, envision, and see the detailed steps to make scrambled, 3-minute, or hard-boiled eggs and how to peel them, then move on to an omelet, eggs Benedict. Every kid and adult should know such basics.

> **Proverbs 14:23**
>
> In all labor, there is profit (mental health is a benefit): But the talk of the lips tends only to penury (staying tied to the mooring is a descent into anxiety).

A person's purpose depends on their talents, skill level, and particularly their likes and dislikes. If all those criteria line up, then you get a direction. It's good to have a medium-term objective in mind so the individual can see how the first and intermediary steps lead to a bigger feasible goal. The slightest movement to the destination activates the mind and reduces anxiety and depression. Once a person embarks on regular steps, no matter how minute, their mental health takes an upswing.

---

4. https://theexplanation.com/compass

5. https://theexplanation.com/compass

27. Bible Proverbs Fix Conduct Issues

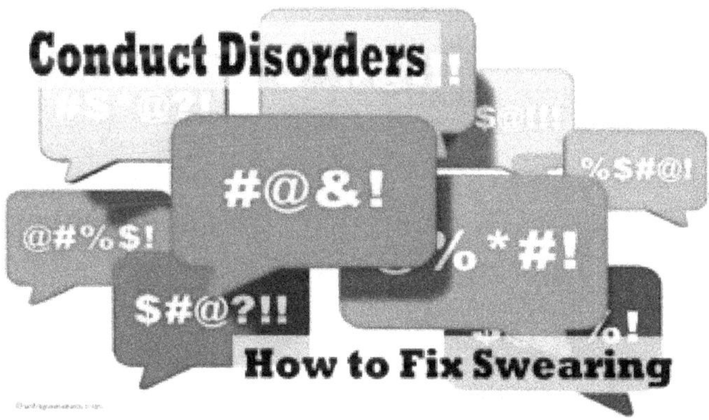

What are Conduct Disorders? And especially, what is their cause? Biological brain or mental mind? How to avoid and heal them.

Prevalence & Nature of Conduct Disorders

In the US Vice Presidential debate, Vance addressed the question of Mental Health and just how widespread it is: "We, unfortunately, have a mental health crisis in this country... (see excerpt from the video below)." It's not the only one. Michel Barnier, the Prime Minister of France, declared 2025 the Mental Health Year in that country.

Let's see the classical analysis of conduct disorders from Nationwide Children's Hospital[1].

> Conduct disorder refers to a group of behavioral and emotional problems characterized by a disregard for others.

1. https://www.nationwidechildrens.org/conditions/conduct-disorders

> Children with conduct disorders have a difficult time following rules and behaving in a socially acceptable way. Their behavior can be hostile and sometimes physically violent.

Note 2 points right from the start.

1. We find children with conduct disorders across all races, cultures, and socioeconomic groups. Sam: Conduct Disorder exists everywhere and is not exclusive to any specific group. We need a global solution.
2. Research has found that children and teens with conduct disorder seem to have an impairment in the frontal lobe of the brain. Sam: This is the article's only mention of biological and neurological causes. I'm not saying neurology doesn't play a part. Indeed, there can be minor or severe brain damage that impairs the mind; that's out of the scope of the *Bible Proverbs Method*. The article goes on to list many EXTERNAL influences:

1. Having experienced abuse, parental rejection, or neglect.
2. Being diagnosed with other psychiatric disorders.
3. Biological parents diagnosed with ADHD, alcohol use disorder, depression, bipolar disorder, or schizophrenia.
4. Poor nutrition.
5. Living in poverty.
6. Maternal psychopathology.
7. Poor parenting/lack of parental involvement.
8. Inconsistent, overly harsh, or otherwise ineffective discipline.
9. Exposure to violence. (society, I'd add sex)
10. Peer delinquency. (society)
11. Having been subjected to physical, sexual, and/or emotional abuse.

12. Lack of adequate parental or other adult supervision.

You must realize that ALL of these causes point to parenting. Here's the scenario. Normally constituted babies and children are NOT born with NOR subject to Conduct Disorders. The nurturing, or rather the poor nurturing, is the cause. That's why I stated that conduct disorders are not kids' problems but parents' and societal problems. That's where the buck starts; this is a generational dilemma. If we want to turn it around, we must impact parental caregiving.

Bible Proverbs Method - Exercise 3 - Conduct

Figure 14. Five aspects of consciousness

Conduct is the third of the five areas of consciousness. Biblically, human conduct has seven parts[2]: Two-faced, free will, behavior, ethics, justice, self-reproach, and forgiveness. The more one of these areas is distorted, the more we'll have conduct disorders.

Specific attitudes, feelings, and actions elaborate on these seven steps. Each of us displays hundreds, probably thousands, of aspects of conduct. This third exercise isolates one specific conduct. It could be alcohol, debt, parents, envy, laziness, poverty, anger, children, pride, wealth, women, adultery, etc. Even those traits are global.

2. https://theexplanation.com/mystery-of-human-conduct-origin-wonders-woes/

Drill down until you get to one specific behavior you can identify and work on for a week. It's your personal choice. If you're unsure, talk with a good friend and ask them to point out some behavior you might not even be aware of that needs improvement.

For this exercise, I've chosen tongue, and to be precise, four-letter words that are obscene. We could also include blasphemous expletives like *Jesus* or *Oh my God*. It seems we have to use them. These phrases get interjected into our dialogue, often without us realizing we're doing it because it becomes so natural.

The sixth aspect of Conduct is self-reproach, seeing ourselves with reality and how we are, not just superficially, via our clothing or hairdo, but in our minds. When we raise our voices and get overheated, we shoot crude interjections out of our mouths faster than we know. Well, it's time to bring such adverse conduct under control, even to a complete stop.

Proverbs 21:23

> Whoso *keeps* (H8104) his mouth and his tongue *keeps* (H8104) his soul from *troubles* (H6869).

There are hundreds, maybe thousands of exercises to keep your mouth and tongue.

Study during the week. Use UnlockBibleMeaning.com

- Troubles (H6869): The translators did not use the word *anxiety*, but the above Proverb could easily express it: Keep your tongue, and it keeps you from anxiety.

H6869

צָרָה tsârâh tsaw-raw'; feminine of H6862 (צַר); tightness (i.e. figuratively, trouble); transitively, a female rival:

KJV - adversary, adversity, affliction, anguish, distress, tribulation, trouble.

- Study the meanings of the word *keep* (H8104). It's the same word God used to tell Adam to *keep* the Garden (Genesis 2:15) and to *keep* the Ten Commandments (Exodus 20:6). Keeping your tongue is in good company. Keep your tongue, and it'll keep you from anxiety.
- Meditate on other verses about the tongue, like Proverbs 15:44: "A wholesome tongue is a tree of life, but perverseness therein is a breach in the spirit." A curse word might be less serious than perverseness; nonetheless, it is perverse to a degree.

If you're a parent using foul language at home, it impacts one person: your child(ren). Don't be surprised when your child exhibits the same disorder as you since kids mimic dad and mom's behavior. This Proverb affects both the younger and older generations and should especially be taken seriously by the latter. The same applies to coaches and anyone who has responsibility for others.

Articles and Quotes about swearing and not swearing

How I Finally Learned To Stop Swearing[3]: Remember you need critical thinking when you read everything. The author of this article goes for hypnotism. Learn what hypnotism is:

"Hypnotherapy works by evoking a deep sense of relaxation before deactivating the area of your brain that handles analytical thinking. Bypassing your critical faculties opens your unconscious mind to the

3. https://www.the-father-hood.com/article/how-i-finally-learned-to-stop-swearing/

power of suggestion. That's the part of the mind that holds onto our old habits, emotions, memories and behaviours," Cameron says, "And if we can reach an agreement with that part of your mind: voila – magic happens." Hypnotherapy might be quicker, but it's precisely this kind of *magic* you must avoid, which can have negative repercussions.

Let *The Explanation* based on the Bible state clearly: never lose control of your mind, and never let someone else take control of your mind. Never let your child lose their mind (which they do during tantrums); this is dangerous because if you don't control your mind, something else might. A word to the wise: you do not want that. Your mind is the most essential commodity you possess; use the correct therapies to beat bad habits, conduct disorders, and anxiety. Use the *Bible Proverbs Method.*

I searched high and low for a psychology article that treated the specific conduct disorder of cussing and couldn't find one that condemned it, except for biblically oriented ones. A study in the National Library of Medicine[4] even showed cussing is an excellent characteristic for reducing stress. It shows that we need critical thinking to separate wisdom from foolishness. Other quotes agree swearing is a no-no.

> The foolish and wicked practice of profane cursing and swearing is a vice so mean and low that every person of sense and character detests and despises it.
>
> –George Washington

Some would say, well, that was over 200 years ago. Here's another quote:

> I was brought up in the Boys' Brigade and grew up not swearing. It's so lovely to behave decently, civilly.

4. https://www.ncbi.nlm.nih.gov/pmc/articles/PMC10171984/

–Jimmy Hill, English football broadcaster

Proverbs 15:23

A man has joy by the answers of his mouth, and a word spoken in due season, how good it is!

Who knows if they swore in Solomon's age? But people certainly do today.

Focus on a word you use, and catch yourself saying it; it's usually just interjected into the sentence. Make a shift from conduct disorder and omit it. Keep it simple, that is, work on one word or phrase. However, you might find all your cussing will come to light; that's even better. By the end of the week, you will have made measurable progress. You're on your way. How do you feel? A little less anxious? Ask yourself why you feel better.

28. Reconnect Friendships in the Phone Era

Ubiquitous cell phones and socialization; How to revitalize amazing sociability.

Social or Asocial

Socialization is the fourth of five aspects[1] attributed to humankind via the ***breath*** *of life*, neshama in Hebrew, which God blew into the first human. How can *The Explanation* affirm this? Because God is social, He put the first humans IN His Garden and always wanted to be WITH them. That's the meaning of Emmanuel: *God with us*. Humans separated themselves from God, and now cell phones are separating humans from one another.

Mind Refreshed means getting over social withdrawal and returning to social bonding. It means curbing the use of cell phones and using the *Bible Proverbs Method* to turn social disengagement around. We're

1. https://theexplanation.com/socialization-rulership-humanity-excels-animals/

choosing one of the five main traits of consciousness, socialization, and focusing on one specific point, cell phone usage, for a week to beat anxiety and stress. Here's our Proverb:

> **Proverbs 18:24**
>
> A man (and woman) that has *friends* (H7453) must shew himself *friendly* (H7489): and there is a *friend* (H157) that sticks closer than a brother.

There are three different words for *friend* in this verse; I leave it to you to go to UnlockBibleMeaning.com[2] to study two of them. We will only look at the first one.

> **H7453**
>
> רֵעַ rêaʻ ray'-ah; or רֵיעַ; from H7462 (רָעָה); an associate (more or less close):
>
> KJV - brother, companion, fellow, friend, husband, lover, neighbour, × (an-) other.

Friendliness extends into all aspects of our lives, from our mates to our children and even our neighborhood. But now, we're not dancing (with Baby), playing, or recreating together as we did in the past. A study reveals[3] the relationship between cell phones and social relationships. We know the harmful effects of another person's phone use in social situations but minimize our own.

Awareness of Degraded Social Relationships

2. https://UnlockBibleMeaning.com

3. https://psnlab.princeton.edu/document/591

Emma, a 28-year-old marketing professional, always prided herself on being productive and connected. She started every morning with her phone in hand, scrolling through emails, checking social media, and catching up on news. Emma thought this routine was an efficient way to start her day. However, over time, she began to notice some unsettling changes. Emma reached for her phone at every free moment: waiting in line for coffee, lunch breaks, and even movie nights with friends. It wasn't just a few minutes here and there; she spent hours daily on her phone.

One day, while out to dinner with her best friend, Emma noticed her friend had been quiet for a while. When she looked up from her phone, her friend was disappointed and asked, "Are you even here?" It hit her hard. She realized she had spent most of the evening scrolling through Instagram instead of engaging with her friend. She felt embarrassed and guilty. That moment lingered in her mind for days.

The tipping point came a few days later when Emma received her weekly screen time report. The number shocked her: an average of 6 hours on her phone daily, with nearly 3 hours spent on social media alone. It was more time than spent reading, exercising, or interacting face-to-face with people she cared about. She realized she was missing out on real-life moments, trading them for mindless scrolling. She felt like she lived more through a screen than in the real world.

Determined to Change Social Relationships

> The only way we'll reclaim our lives from our devices is if we create boundaries... if we don't set up our own boundaries, our technology will set them for us.
>
> –Arianna Huffington

Determined to make a change, Emma set some ground rules for herself. She started small, deciding to keep her phone in her bag during meals and setting time limits for her social media apps. Emma also created a *no-phone* rule for the first hour after waking up and an hour before bed, filling that time with other activities like reading and journaling. To her surprise, after just a week, she noticed a difference. She felt more present during conversations, more relaxed in the mornings, and more connected to the world around her.

It wasn't easy for Emma to break the habit entirely, but with each day, Emma felt more in control. Her relationships improved, she had more time for hobbies, and most importantly, she felt she was reclaiming her life from the digital world.

Exercises to Fight Social Withdrawal

These are designed to help break the habit of overusing a cell phone and foster real-life connections:

1. Phone-Free Meal Challenge

How it Works: When you go out to eat with friends or family, make a pact that everyone must place their phones in the middle of the table, face down. The first person to pick up their phone has to either pay for the meal or do a small dare or task chosen by the group.

Purpose: This exercise encourages you to focus on the people around you and enjoy the experience without distractions. Over time, it helps reinforce the habit of putting your phone away during meals and being more present in social situations.

2. 30-Minute Walk-and-Talk

How it Works: Instead of texting or chatting over social media, invite a friend or family member for a 30-minute walk outdoors. Leave your phone behind or on silent, and use the time to catch up and enjoy each other's company without digital interruptions.

Purpose: Walking while talking provides a healthier and more engaging way to socialize than texting or messaging. This exercise promotes physical activity and strengthens relationships by allowing for focused, meaningful conversation.

3. The 24-Hour Phone-Free Challenge

How it Works: Pick one day of the week, such as a Saturday or Sunday, to go completely phone-free. Spend the day doing activities with friends or family that don't require digital devices, such as hiking, board games, or visiting a museum. Make it a group challenge, and plan phone-free activities with others.

Purpose: Spending a whole day without your phone allows you to reconnect with the people and experiences around you. Realizing how much time you usually spend on your device can be eye-opening, and the experience can inspire you to incorporate more screen-free time into your routine.

Read the article The Impact of Mobile Phone Use on Social Interactions[4]. Mobile phone usage reduces face-to-face interaction time, impacting emotional well-being. Heavy phone users tend to experience lower satisfaction with social interactions.

Put down your cell phone and face social withdrawal with courage and perseverance. Decide to do it with a family member or friend. Do it for a week, two weeks, or a month, and your anxiety will diminish; you'll be a better person.

4. https://link.springer.com/article/10.1007/s40429-022-00445-4

29. Workplace Diligence: Success Guide

Mastering diligence is vital in all life aspects and fundamental to mental health management—the proven way to long-term success.

Diligence and Rulership

Diligence is the fifth exercise for the *Bible Proverbs Method*;[1] it relates to one aspect of rulership[2], the fifth characteristic of consciousness: diligence. Within the vastness of diligence, we will focus on your line of work and one specific drill for increasing it.

These exercises last one week, and here is the Proverb we'll be concentrating on.

Proverbs 12:24

1. https://theexplanation.com/bible-proverbs-therapy-for-anxiety-onlybenefits/

2. https://theexplanation.com/socialization-rulership-humanity-excels-animals/

> The hand of the *diligent* (H2742) shall bear rule: but the slothful shall be under *tribute* (H4522).

Do you see that rulership is the result of diligence? There's a direct relationship between diligence and consciousness. Animals accomplish what they're programmed to do: gathering food, self-preservation, or searching for a mate. Not so with humans; we must apply perseverance to our endeavors.

Either we run our lives with reasoning, purpose, conduct, socialization, and rulership, or our lives will run us, as the Proverb says. Look at the meaning of *tribute* in Hebrew at UnlockBibleMeaning.com[3]

H4522

מַס maç mas; or מִס; from H4549 (מָסַס); properly, a burden (as causing to faint), i.e. a tax in the form of forced labor:

KJV - **discomfited**, levy, task(-master), tribute(-tary).

H4549

מָסַס mâçaç maw-sas'; a primitive root; to liquefy; figuratively, to waste (with disease), to faint (with fatigue, fear or grief):

KJV - **discourage**, faint, be loosed, **melt (away)**, refuse, × utterly.

To not be diligent is to be discouraged, discomfited, in other words, anxious, and worried. Becoming more diligent is a way to beat anxiety and increase your mental health. Here's Josh's story; apply it to your situation.

---

3. https://UnlockBibleMeaning.com

Diligence Leads to Success

Josh, a 32-year-old accountant, had always felt indifferent about his job. He saw his work as something he had to do, not something he wanted to do. Every day felt the same—long hours behind a desk, endless spreadsheets, and a mountain of paperwork. He clocked in and out with minimal engagement, doing just enough to meet deadlines but never feeling pride or passion for his work. He often daydreamed about switching careers or starting his own business but never took any real action.

Then, one day, his manager, Sarah, pulled him aside for a performance review. She noticed his lack of enthusiasm and mentioned how his productivity had been declining. She didn't reprimand him but instead asked, "Josh, do you even enjoy what you're doing?" The question, though simple, hit Josh harder than he expected. He realized that his lack of motivation wasn't just affecting his job—it was bleeding into other areas of his life. He felt stuck, stagnant, and dissatisfied, but quitting wasn't an option due to financial obligations.

That night, Josh reflected deeply on Sarah's question. He knew he needed a change, but maybe not a career change—just a **change in attitude**. Josh decided to make a conscious effort to approach his work differently. Instead of focusing on what he disliked, he searched for **aspects of the job he could appreciate**. Josh **set small goals for himself**, like improving his efficiency with Excel or mastering new accounting software. He also arrived 15 minutes earlier daily to **organize his tasks** and set a clear plan.

As weeks passed, Josh began to notice a **shift in his mindset**. He had become more diligent; the same tasks that once felt monotonous now gave him a sense of accomplishment as he completed them with increasing skill. He also began engaging more with his colleagues, offering help when needed and suggesting ideas for streamlining processes. Surprisingly, this led to more positive feedback from his manager and peers.

Josh didn't magically fall in love with accounting but found satisfaction in developing diligence by taking ownership of his attitude and approach. His career didn't change overnight, but his newfound work ethic opened doors to promotions and greater responsibility. More importantly, he felt a renewed sense of purpose, knowing he could choose how he approached life's challenges—whether at work or beyond.

> There are no secrets to success. It is the result of preparation, hard work, and learning from failure.
>
> –Henry Ford

Ford, the American industrialist, reinforces the importance of preparation, diligence, and perseverance for success rather than relying on shortcuts.

There are many tips to take away from Josh's example, some of which I highlighted above. Keeping to the theme of this book, *Mind Refreshed*, is exactly what Josh did. He reflected deeply, which resulted in a change of attitude; this is mind-activating diligence, a specific aspect of the rulership sphere of consciousness.

From the various translations (Key 1 to Master Biblical Hebrew[4]) of the Hebrew word for *diligence* and its root (Key 6[5]) in Pro. 12:24, we see the meanings: *decision*, *bestir*, *determine*, *move*; we need to become sharper threshing instruments for an abundant harvest.

H2742

4. https://theexplanation.com/key-1-biblical-hebrew-words-have-various-meanings/

5. https://theexplanation.com/key-6-biblical-hebrew-word-roots-unlock-bible-meaning/

חָרוּץ chărûwts khaw-roots'; or חָרֻץ; passive participle of H2782 (חָרַץ); properly, incised or (active) incisive; hence (as noun masculine or feminine) a trench (as dug), gold (as mined), a threshing-sledge (having sharp teeth); (figuratively) determination; also eager:

KJV - decision, diligent, (fine) gold, pointed things, sharp, threshing instrument, wall.

H2782

חָרַץ chârats khaw-rats'; a primitive root; properly, to point sharply, i.e. (literally) to wound; figuratively, to be alert, to decide:

KJV - bestir self, decide, decree, determine, maim, move.

How to Develop Diligence

You're probably not an accountant; apply these principles to your work habits. Don't overload yourself; focus on the easiest one this week and ingrain it until you're comfortable with it.

1. Set Clear, Daily Goals

How it works: At the start of each day, list three to five essential tasks you need to accomplish. Prioritize them and break larger tasks into manageable steps.

Purpose: This helps you stay focused and organized and ensures steady progress. Daily completion of these goals builds momentum and reinforces a diligent work habit.

Tip: Use time-blocking to schedule focused periods for each task, which enhances productivity.

2. Eliminate Distractions for Focused Work Time

How it works: Dedicate uninterrupted work periods, such as using the Pomodoro technique (25 minutes of work followed by a short break). Turn off phone notifications or use apps that block distractions.

Purpose: Diligence thrives on focus. You can concentrate on your tasks more efficiently by eliminating distractions, resulting in higher-quality work and faster progress.

Tip: Start small, with one or two focused sessions per day, and gradually increase as your attention span improves.

Diligence Definitely Improves Mental Health

Don't take my word for it. The Bible says it, and psychology studies reveal its positive effects on mental well-being. This article equates diligence with grit. Grit and Achievement: New Perspectives on the Role of Diligence[6]

The paper provides a meta-analysis of how perseverance, a critical component of diligence, relates to success in both personal and professional life, suggesting that sustained effort can overcome various obstacles. Grit, Well-Being, and Positive Psychological Outcomes[7]: Researchers have offered evidence on the benefits of grittiness for well-being in diverse contexts, which link to higher levels of life satisfaction among many groups.

---

6. https://www.frontiersin.org/journals/psychology/articles/10.3389/fpsyg.2020.545526/full
7. https://www.researchgate.net/publication/284187126_Grit_and_Different_Aspects_of_Well-Being_Direct_and_Indirect_Relationships_via_Sense_of_Coherence_and_Authenticity

Diligence is a Proverb's principle that, when applied, moves us out of anxiety and into a more satisfied and mentally stable life

30. Consciousness: Science or Bible?

We all do conscious reasoning. And therein lies the problem: We all think from different foundations, resulting in confusion.

Why so much Chaos with Conscious Reasoning?

The first five exercises finished our first cycle through the five aspects of consciousness: Reasoning, Purpose, Conduct, Socialization, and Rulership. We'll always swing back and restart the cycle. Remember, these five elements that make us in the image of God contain every single factor that defines humankind.

Exercise 6 of the *Bible Proverbs Method* is related to conscious reasoning. Within reasoning, the method focuses on one precise point for a week. In our first round of the five phases, we zeroed in on reasoning about a Higher Power. This week, we want to examine whether this Higher Power gave us a foundational document.

You can personalize your treatment by choosing another specificity of conscious reasoning with the exercises. But remember, your focus and exercises must help you regain or fortify your mental health using a Proverb. At UnlockBibleMeaning.com[1], search for subjects related to reasoning, such as *word*, *instruction*, and *hear*, and find your weekly Proverb to work on. More details on the personalization of the *Bible Proverbs Method* are at this link[2] or in the last chapter of this book—our Proverb for this week.

Proverbs 30:5

Every word of God is pure: he is a shield to them that put their trust in him.

Reasoning Exercise

This week's exercise will compare two documents related to the discovery of consciousness. The goal is to realize that **the document that reveals the answer to consciousness is the foundational document for conscious reasoning.** *Every word of God is pure.* I advance this argument because the whereabouts of consciousness is an over 400-year enigma that science is not resolving; indeed, the waters are getting murkier than ever.

Toward a Taxonomy of Explanations and Implications

The complete document by Dr. Robert Kuhn[3] is about 1100 pages long. His opening comment lays the groundwork for his monumental undertaking to document the scholarly views of consciousness.

---

1. https://unlockbiblemeaning.com
2. https://docs.google.com/spreadsheets/d/1UVmEQc5xB9v8rCEL36CZpgFRdhKfHXNh0IxKJZoN8do/edit?usp=sharing
3. https://www.sciencedirect.com/science/article/pii/S0079610723001128?via%3Dihub

> Explanations of consciousness abound, and the radical diversity of theories is telling. Explanations, or theories, are said to work at astonishingly divergent orders of magnitude and putative realms of reality. My purpose here must be humble: collect and categorize, not assess and adjudicate. Seek insights, not answers.

I'm very thankful for this massive work and acknowledge Dr. Kuhn's thoroughness and integrity of presentation. It does reveal the radical diversity in the most fundamental subject of humans: How can flesh and bones think and have feelings?

> I have followed consciousness studies in its various forms for my entire life. My PhD is in neurophysiology (thalamocortical evoked potentials). I am creator and host of *Closer To Truth*, the long-running public television series and web resource on science and philosophy, roughly one-third of which focuses on consciousness and brain/mind topics. I have discussed consciousness with over 200 scientists and philosophers who work on or think about consciousness and related fields. Closer To Truth YouTube[4]; Closer To Truth website[5].

You can listen to this vast diversity of scientists' and philosophers' ideas on his website. Here is a graphic representing the categories and myriad ideas.

4. https://www.sciencedirect.com/science/article/pii/S0079610723001128?via%3Dihub#bib167

5. https://www.sciencedirect.com/science/article/pii/S0079610723001128?via%3Dihub#bib166

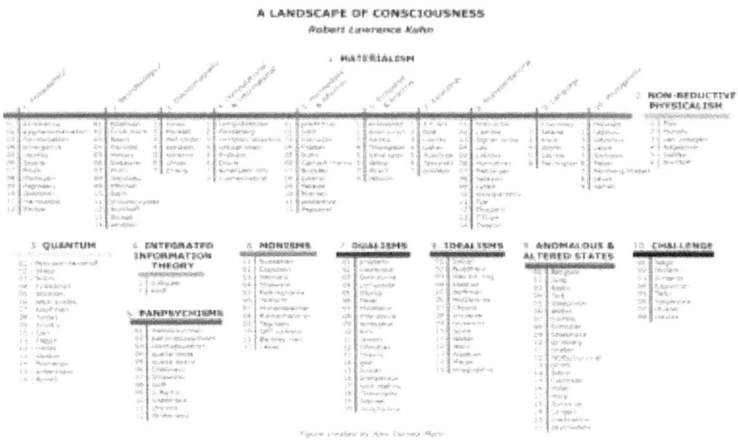

Figure 15. Landscape of consciousness

Conscious reasoning of thinkers tells us that consciousness exists. I could tell you to study all the above concepts and figure it out from that foundation. You will take ten lifetimes and be no further ahead. Let's look at another source.

Conscious Reasoning Based on the Bible

In the first exercise about conscious reasoning, we showed an All-Powerful Higher Power. This second exercise goes one step further, revealing He has published the revelation of what it is to be human, the foremost element being that each of us is impregnated with consciousness.

This book, *Mind Refreshed,* already developed this conscious reasoning, but I want to return to it here to show three straightforward Bible verses in contrast to 1100 pages of confused reasoning.

Genesis 2:7

> And the LORD God formed man of the dust of the ground, and breathed into his nostrils the *breath* (H5397) of life; and man became a living soul.

Breath of life is *neshama* in Hebrew, much more than just the air we breathe. Here's how we know.

> **H5397**
>
> נְשָׁמָה n^{e}shâmâh nesh-aw-maw'; from H5395 (נָשַׁם); a puff, i.e. wind, angry or vital breath, divine inspiration, intellect. or (concretely) an animal:
>
> KJV - blast, (that) breath(-eth), inspiration, soul, spirit.

The Creation of the first human reveals breath-neshama, which includes *inspiration* and *spirit*. That's dualism; the physical and non-physical realms are reality. Until science and all the other domains consider this fact, we'll have reams of half-baked knowledge and thousands of pages of unconscious reasoning.

What Does Neshama Confer On Humans?

Let's elaborate on this non-material aspect of neshama.

> **Job 32:8**
>
> But there is a spirit in man: and the *inspiration* (H5397-neshama) of the Almighty gives them *understanding* (H995).

This is the Almighty, the All-Powerful's Neshama, which He shares with us. It alone imparts *understanding* to humans. This commodity encompasses several qualities that science has no clue about: where they came from, how we acquire them, and where they're located. Here's a list of those traits conferred on us by God's Neshama.

H995

בִּין bîyn bene; a primitive root; to separate mentally (or distinguish), i.e.(generally) understand:

KJV - attend, consider, be cunning, **diligently**, direct, **discern**, eloquent, **feel**, **inform**, **instruct**, have **intelligence**, know, look well to, mark, **perceive**, be prudent, regard, (can) skill(-full), **teach**, **think**, (cause, make to, get, give, have) understand(-ing), view, (deal) **wise**(-ly, man).

Consider all these as characteristics of *understanding*. Each human has God's Neshama, which allows us to think, have feelings, discern, and be wise.

With two verses and a comprehension of the Hebrew word *understanding-bain*, we've used the Bible with conscious reasoning to solve the age-old problem of consciousness. It took just over 200 words, in contrast to 1100 pages of gobbledygook ideas.

So you decide if the Bible, the Scriptures, God's inspired Words are the foundation of conscious reasoning. Every Word of God is pure as Pro. 30:5 states. Nowhere else do we find a concise and straightforward revelation of what consciousness is.

Conscious Reasoning Tells Us Who Possesses Consciousness

I could end this expose about consciousness here, but I want to add a final point where science and philosophers are entirely in the dark. Who or what possesses consciousness?

Joshua 11:14

And all the spoil of these cities, and the cattle, the children of Israel took for a prey unto themselves; but every man they smote with the edge of the sword, until they had destroyed them, neither left they any to *breathe* (H5397-neshama).

The Israelites destroyed everything with neshama, but they took all the animals to themselves. The limpid conclusion, using conscious reasoning, is humans ALONE possess neshama.

As *The Explanation* has developed throughout *Mind-Body Problem Solved* and its workbook, *Mind Refreshed*, this portion of God's Neshama makes humans in God's Image. Humans, on their minimal level, have the same mental qualities as their All-Powerful Maker: Reasoning[6], Purpose[7], Conduct[8], Socialization, and Rulership[9].

Proverbs 1:1-2

1 The proverbs of Solomon the son of David, king of Israel;

2 To know wisdom and instruction; to perceive the words of understanding;

Not only Proverbs, but the entire Word of God is the foundation of all knowledge. God gave us conscious reasoning and wants us to use it correctly. When we straighten out our thinking and correctly differentiate between Godly and worldly wisdom, we'll become wiser in our understanding and, by the same token, reduce our stress and anxiety, leading to much improved mental health.

---

6. https://theexplanation.com/mystery-of-human-conduct-origin-wonders-woes/

7. https://theexplanation.com/unraveling-purpose-inside-scoop-unique-humans/

8. https://theexplanation.com/mystery-of-human-conduct-origin-wonders-woes/

9. https://theexplanation.com/socialization-rulership-humanity-excels-animals/

31. Wealth: Is It Life's Sole Purpose?

The Internet promotes a plethora of get-rich-quick schemes. Is this a good idea? Why do we crave wealth? A better way.

Wealth is Not the Main Purpose of Life

Money and wealth are concerns, even significant purposes in our lives. Whatever situation we're in, we need money. What role should shooting to be rich play in our lives?

This is the seventh weekly exercise for the *Bible Proverbs Method.*

So, let's ask, Is God rich? If He is, then we have the answer to our question. Of course, God is wealthy. But here's the all-important follow-up question? Does He hoard this wealth for Himself? No.

Psalm 115:16

The heaven, even the heavens, are the LORD's: but the earth has he given to the children of men.

Sharing Our Wealth is Our Fundamental Purpose

God shares His wealth. His purpose is not wealth for wealth's sake. It's wealth He transmits for the uplifting benefit of others. When we look at Genesis 1, a sumptuous description of the planet Earth we live on, and consider our environment, we understand how God has put His wealth at the disposal of the children of men.

Here's our Proverb for this week. Study it at UnlockBibleMeaning.com[1]. Meditate, pray, and find related verses, contexts, and stories revealing the principle of sharing one's wealth, including not just finances but time and energy, for the benefit of others.

Proverbs 11:24-26

24 There is that scatters, and yet increases; and there is that withholds more than is meet, but it tends to poverty.

25 The liberal soul shall be made fat: and he that waters shall be watered also himself.

26 He that withholds corn, the people shall curse him: but blessing shall be upon the head of him that sells it.

Exemplary Sharing of Wealth

How Maria became a liberal soul: In her late thirties, she was a single mother of two who discovered a profound purpose in life through her journey to support her family. After her divorce, Maria realized she had

1. https://UnlockBibleMeaning.com

to find a way to provide for her kids and herself. She had previously worked a few part-time jobs but now wanted something stable and fulfilling. So, she took a leap of faith, pursued a course in web design, and gradually built a small freelancing business.

At first, Maria's goal was purely financial – she needed to cover rent, school fees, and daily expenses. However, as her skills improved and her client base grew, she earned more than anticipated. With her newfound financial stability, Maria began to experience a shift in her mindset. She realized how much she valued the journey – from acquiring skills to running her own business – and recognized the immense empowerment this brought her life.

Then, Maria decided she wanted others to experience the same sense of purpose and fulfillment. She started by reaching out to a few women in her community who faced financial challenges and lacked direction like her. Maria organized informal training sessions, sharing her knowledge of web design and lessons on entrepreneurship, self-worth, and resilience. Her sessions grew in popularity, and she soon mentored a group of aspiring women eager to create their own paths.

As Maria's earnings increased, so did her generosity. She reinvested much of her income into these women's dreams, helping them cover initial expenses for online courses, software, and marketing. She saw her earnings not just as a way to live comfortably but as a means to inspire and uplift others. Through her support, several of her mentees landed their first freelance gigs, and some even launched small businesses, making enough to support themselves and their families.

Maria's financial success allowed her to build a network of women who felt they had a purpose, breaking the cycle of dependency they once felt trapped in. Her story is a powerful example of a woman who didn't just seek to earn money but also used it as a tool for creating positive change and helping others find their own purpose and self-reliance.

> The purpose of life is not to be happy. It is to be useful, to be honorable, to be compassionate, to have it make some difference that you have lived and lived well.
>
> –Ralph Waldo Emerson

Exercises to Develop Sharing Wealth

That's the purpose of wealth. It doesn't come overnight. Depending on what finances, time, and energy you can share right now, make it a short—or long-term purpose. Here are three practical exercises to get you underway.

1. Daily Acts of Kindness

Set aside a specific amount of money or time each day for small acts of generosity. For example, buy a coffee for a stranger, donate a few dollars to a charity, or spend 15 minutes volunteering online. These small acts build the habit of giving and make sharing a natural part of your routine.

2. Volunteer Your Skills Weekly

Commit to sharing your skills or knowledge with others once a week. For example, if you're skilled in graphic design, offer to create a logo for a local non-profit, or if you're good at teaching, tutor someone who needs academic help. Skill-based volunteering lets you contribute time in ways that are meaningful and effective.

3. Monthly Reflection and Goal Setting

At the end of each month, spend some time reflecting on the impact of your sharing efforts. Ask yourself: What did I give this month? How did it make a difference? What would I like to try next month? Setting small goals for the upcoming month keeps sharing intentional and meaningful.

Proverbs 22:9

He that has a bountiful eye shall be blessed; for he gives of his bread to the poor.

Proverbs 23:4-5

4 Labour not to be rich: cease from your own wisdom.

5 Will you set your eyes upon that which is not? for riches certainly make themselves wings; they fly away as an eagle toward heaven.

We make a living by what we get, but we make a life by what we give.

–Winston Churchill

Five weeks ago, we focused on our passions and skills[2] to determine what we really want to accomplish with our lives. This exercise focuses on sharing the results of our purpose with others. When we align these two fundamentals and put them into practice, the benefits for ourselves and others are multiple. In the context of *Mind Refreshed*, conquering anxiety is a guaranteed benefit.

2. https://theexplanation.com/bible-proverbs-therapy-for-anxiety-onlybenefits/

32. Help Kids Follow Instructions Better!

Using your mind correctly will transform your parenting into raising children who follow instructions. Three exercises to practice.

Nurturing Our Children's Conduct

The first seven *Bible Proverbs Method* exercises focused on healing. But we must not forget the importance of nurturing, the preventive method of excellence for staving off anxiety, stress, and other mental health issues. And nurturing starts at birth with caring parents; this is thoughtful and continued devotion to the new life parents bring into the world.

Only with proper nurturing can we expect a newborn to develop into a mentally stable child, adolescent, and adult. Beating anxiety and mental illness starts in the cradle. This lack of nurturing begs questions about proper dating, couples, compatibility, maturity, marriage, and parenting, but those are other subjects.

Focus on How To Follow Instructions

This Chapter is the eighth exercise of the *Bible Proverbs Method.* The focus is on *conduct,* and the specific point is *following instructions.* As parents, you need to discuss which specific area you want to work on and find the appropriate exercises. Here's our Proverb for the week for nurturing decent conduct in our children: precisely how to follow instructions.

> **Proverbs 1:8**
>
> My son, *hear* (H8085) the *instruction* (H4148) of your father, and forsake not the law of your mother.

Hear is such a simple word in English. The Biblical Hebrew incorporates much deeper meaning.

> **H8085**
>
> שָׁמַע shâmaʻ shaw-mah'; a primitive root; to hear intelligently (often with implication of attention, obedience, etc.; causatively, to tell, etc.):
>
> KJV - × attentively, call (gather) together, × carefully, × certainly, **consent**, consider, be **content**, declare, × diligently, **discern**, give ear, (cause to, let, make to) hear(-ken, tell), × indeed, listen, make (a) noise, (be) **obedient**, obey, perceive, (make a) proclaim(-ation), publish, regard, report, shew (forth), (make a) sound, × surely, tell, **understand**, whosoever (heareth), witness.

I've emboldened a few translations to draw your attention to aspects to incorporate when you teach your children to follow instructions. Help them understand the why; this discernment will cause them to consent to obey. This week, study those words in their various contexts throughout the Bible and see their relationship with how to follow instructions. A further study involves a deeper meaning of *instruction* (H4145). Use the Bible tools at UnlockBibleMeaning.com[1] to expound these concepts. Remember that the Proverb means to follow the instructions of both father and mother.

Parental Example of Teaching How to Follow Instructions

As loving and mindful parents, Daniel and Jessica prioritized nurturing their children, Noah, 10, and Emma, 12, with care, structure, and affection. They understood that teaching their children to follow instructions and act responsibly required patience, guidance, and a deep sense of connection. Their goal was to build a foundation of trust and respect, helping Noah and Emma understand the importance of their choices and actions.

Daniel and Jessica set aside time each evening after dinner to discuss their day with Noah and Emma. During these conversations, they encouraged the children to share their feelings, achievements, and challenges. They created a safe space by actively listening, where their children felt valued and understood. Daniel often said, "Your thoughts matter, and we're here to help you grow," reinforcing the idea that following their instructions wasn't only about obedience but mutual respect and trust.

The parents used a gentle approach to follow instructions, offering explanations rather than simply giving orders. For example, if Noah

1. https://UnlockBibleMeaning.com

resisted completing his homework, Jessica patiently explained how consistent study habits would build skills and confidence. Similarly, if Emma felt discouraged about helping with household chores, her father reminded her how each family member's contribution helped their household run smoothly.

Through these nurturing practices, Noah and Jessica learned to respect their parents' guidance without fear and to understand its value. Daniel and Jessica's love, consistency, and dedication instilled in their children a strong sense of responsibility, respect, and integrity—qualities that would guide them well beyond childhood.

Exercises for How to Follow Instructions

Here are three age-appropriate exercises for parents to help children follow instructions that foster understanding, respect, and responsibility.

1. Clear Instructions with "Why" Explanations

- **How It Works:** When giving instructions, take a moment to explain the reasoning behind them. For example, instead of just saying, "Clean your room," say, "Please clean your room so you have a tidy space to study and play." Encourage questions so your child understands why the task is essential.
- **Goal:** This approach helps your child see obedience as a thoughtful response rather than mere compliance. Understanding the purpose behind instructions encourages them to follow through with intention and respect.

2. Routine and Responsibility Chart

- **How It Works:** Create a weekly chart with tasks like homework, chores, and personal goals. Review it together at the beginning of each week, and let your child check off completed tasks. Celebrate their progress and discuss any challenges they faced.

- **Goal:** This routine reinforces structure and accountability. It encourages children to take ownership of their responsibilities and understand that fulfilling tasks as they follow instructions has positive outcomes, promoting consistent behavior.

3. Listening and Reflecting Exercise

- **How It Works:** Practice a "listening check-in" where you give your child an instruction, and they repeat it back to confirm they understood. For example, "Can you please set the table for dinner?" followed by their response, "I'll set the table for dinner."
- **Goal:** This exercise reinforces active listening, ensuring your child understands and commits to the instructions. It also helps them develop the habit of acknowledging tasks clearly, supporting better follow-through.

Discipline is the bridge between goals and accomplishment.

– Jim Rohn

Following father's and mother's instructions is a foundational part of discipline, which ultimately helps children achieve goals and succeed in their endeavors.

Parents shouldn't have to repeatedly ask their children the same things. Doing so denotes a lack of listening, obedience, and respect. By persevering with practical Biblical methods, you can help your children learn the essential life practice of following instructions.

More importantly, through these experiences, you'll be preparing your child's mind for their future life—a life that will not be problem-free but where they'll be able to cope, possess mental stability, and beat anxiety.

33. Social Bonding Starts in Babyhood

Family social bonding is vital to prepare for future marriage and interconnections with friends, colleagues, and strangers.

Social bonding is the reason God established the family. It is fundamental to society's structure and functioning. It refers to the connections and relationships individuals form with others, fostering trust, cooperation, and mutual support. These bonds are crucial in shaping individual behavior, group dynamics, and societal progress. They are the source and outcome of "Love your neighbor as yourself."

Socialization[1] is the fourth of the five aspects of consciousness. This week's *Bible Proverbs Method* is Exercise 9, and it focuses on one point of social bonding: Parents reading to their young kids to build social interactions from the very start of life. This practice is the vital nurturing of the younger generation to prepare adults with less anxiety and stable mental health. Our Proverb for this week is:

1. https://theexplanation.com/socialization-rulership-humanity-excels-animals/

Proverbs 17:6

> Children's children are the crown of old men; and the glory of children are their fathers.

This Proverb establishes social bonding over three generations. It is an ode to family relationships and attachment to the family structure of society. Mental health starts here. For children, nothing is more essential than getting a solid start in life. This week, focus your Bible study, using UnlockBibleMeaning.com[2], on socialization among families. The Bible has good and bad examples: draw the lessons from each. Drill down to one action you can work on this week as a parent. I've chosen reading to your kids; you can choose whatever is needed and helpful, but choose and do something.

Example of Social Bonding

Jim and Sally intentionally teach their children, Liam (3) and Olivia (5), the importance of social bonding, equipping them with emotional tools and confidence to navigate life. They prioritize creating a nurturing home environment with love, structure, and meaningful interactions.

One of their favorite bonding activities is reading bedtime stories together. Every evening, Jim and Sally take turns reading to Liam and Olivia. For example, Sally might choose a story about friendship, like *Frog and Toad Are Friends*, to emphasize themes of cooperation and empathy. She pauses to ask questions like, "How do you think Frog felt when Toad helped him?"

This approach helps Olivia and Liam develop emotional intelligence and recognize feelings in themselves and others. On the other hand, Jim loves adding dramatic voices to characters, keeping the atmosphere

2. https://unlockbiblemeaning.com

light and engaging. The storytelling reinforces vocabulary and listening skills and strengthens the family bond through shared laughter and imaginative exploration.

In another area, Jim and Sally model calm behavior during stressful situations to prepare Liam and Olivia for managing anxiety. For instance, when Liam spills his juice and becomes visibly upset, Jim reassures him by saying, "It's okay; accidents happen. Let's clean it up together." Liam learns that mistakes are manageable and not something to fear. Additionally, Sally encourages both children to express their feelings. She might say, "Olivia, you seem upset. Do you want to tell me why?" This open communication fosters trust and emotional security.

To promote social skills, Jim and Sally arrange playdates with other families. They coach Liam and Olivia on sharing toys and taking turns. When challenges arise, like a disagreement over a toy, Jim helps them navigate the conflict by encouraging compromise, saying, "Let's find a way to take turns so everyone has fun."

Jim and Sally create a foundation of love, trust, and resilience through these everyday practices. Their dedication to reading and emotional validation strengthens family bonds and equips Liam and Olivia with lifelong tools to handle relationships and anxiety confidently.

Exercises for Social Bonding

1. Family Storytime

What to do: Dedicate time each day to reading books together. Choose stories with engaging pictures and themes that encourage interaction, like asking questions or pointing out objects.

Why it works: Reading together fosters closeness and helps children feel secure. Discussing the story encourages communication, strengthens vocabulary, and develops empathy as kids learn to relate to characters.

2. Sensory Play Adventures

What to do: Create sensory bins or activities using materials like sand, water, playdough, or rice. Let your child explore while parents join in to build structures, pour and scoop, or make patterns together.

Why it works: Engaging in sensory play as a team encourages collaboration and builds trust. Parents modeling curiosity and creativity inspire kids to feel safe and supported in exploring the world.

3. Family Dance Party

What to do: Turn on some favorite songs and dance together, relaxed and playfully. Include actions like clapping, stomping, or twirling that kids can easily mimic.

Why it works: Dancing encourages physical closeness, joy, and laughter, all releasing bonding hormones like oxytocin. Following simple movements also builds social skills like turn-taking and imitation.

Keep activities age-appropriate and flexible to match your child's energy and attention span. Celebrate small efforts and emphasize fun over perfection. Use these moments to model positive interactions, showing love and care in a relaxed setting.

> In every conceivable manner, the family is the link to our past, bridge to our future.
>
> – Alex Haley, author of Roots

Haley emphasizes the intergenerational connection and the role of the family in shaping both personal history and the future: it hearkens back to and emphasizes this week's Proverb.

Psychology Recommends Social Bonding

Psychology has come to realize the importance of social bonding from the earliest age. Read these articles for the latest research in this field. Remember to do so with a discerning Biblical eye. God's Wisdom through Proverbs is the basis of actions and thoughts. Not everything we see in print is Gospel truth. Prove all things.

What you need to know about parent-child attachment - UNICEF

This article[3] emphasizes how bonding with children from infancy lays the foundation for emotional security, resilience, and self-confidence. It provides actionable tips for parents, such as responding to a child's cues, engaging in play, and fostering open communication.

Powerful Interactions: Building Relationships Through Everyday Activities - NAEYC (National Association for the Education of Young Children)

This piece focuses on fostering strong parent-child relationships[4] and introduces the "Powerful Interactions" framework. It highlights how small, intentional interactions during routine activities can strengthen bonds and promote learning.

These articles add valid, researched psychological weight to the role of parents in laying the groundwork for their children's social and

3. https://www.unicef.org/parenting/child-care/what-you-need-know-about-parent-child-attachment

4. https://www.naeyc.org/resources/pubs/tyc/aug2018/promoting-powerful-interactions

emotional well-being through consistent care, interactive play, and exposure to social environments. These efforts not only strengthen the parent child bond but also equip the child with tools to build healthy relationships and navigate life with reduced anxiety.

34. Teach Organization: A Lifelong Gift

Organization is a necessity at any age. However, the best time to learn to manage oneself and one's possessions is as early as possible.

This is exercise 10, the last of the book *Mind Refreshed*[1]: Helping Kids Learn Organization. These exercises are examples of the *Bible Proverbs Method (BPM)*. Understand that your peace of mind comes from an equilibrium of five areas that cover your life: your Reasoning, Purpose[2], Conduct, Socialization, and Rulership[3]. The more these areas are aligned, the more peace you'll have; the less they're aligned, the more anxiety you'll have.

Organization Proverb and Example

1. *https://theexplanation.com/transform*

2. https://theexplanation.com/mystery-of-human-conduct-origin-wonders-woes/

3. https://theexplanation.com/socialization-rulership-humanity-excels-animals/

When we teach the principles of Proverbs during childhood, we nurture, and for those with mental illness, we heal. To overcome mental ill-health, we must apply both because this is the only way to prepare the future generation in a better state than we are today. Here's our Proverb for this week. Study at UnlockBibleMeaning.com[4], there are many passages and stories about managing one's environment.

Proverbs 24:27

> Prepare your work without, and make it fit for yourself in the field; and afterwards build your house.

This verse about organization includes many principles about life. It prioritizes exercising a solid profession before considering serious relationships that could lead to marriage or children. Here, it's the organization of agriculture fields, but find a specific point you can work on for at least one week. Teaching children aged 3-5 about making their bed or organizing their room, an age-appropriate task, is a valuable life skill that fosters independence, responsibility, and cognitive development. At this impressionable age, children are developing habits and foundational skills that can significantly impact their future behavior and approach to challenges.

Jim and Judy were proud parents to their lively 5-year-old twins, Noah and Suriya. While the twins brought boundless joy to their lives, the chaos of scattered toys, misplaced belongings, and undone chores often overwhelmed their home. Determined to teach their children the value of organization, Jim and Judy decided to make it a fun family journey.

They started with the twins' room. Jim built colorful shelves and bins labeled with pictures to help Noah and Suriya know where their toys belonged. The family turned cleanup time into a playful race with a

4. https://unlockbiblemeaning.com

timer and cheers of encouragement. The twins quickly learned to sort their blocks, dolls, and art supplies into their designated spots.

Next, Judy introduced a chore chart with stickers, creating a simple system to teach responsibility. Noah loved watering plants, while Suriya became the "laundry helper," eagerly tossing dirty clothes into the hamper. Completing tasks earned the twins stars, which could be traded for small rewards like choosing a family movie night.

To instill routine, the parents created a morning and bedtime checklist with illustrations, guiding the twins through brushing their teeth, making their beds, and tidying up. By turning these tasks into engaging habits, Jim and Judy helped Noah and Suriya embrace responsibility without feeling overwhelmed.

Over time, the twins began to take pride in their organized room and completed chores. Judy smiled as she saw Noah helping Suriya fold her blanket and Suriya reminding Noah to pick up his blocks. Their journey wasn't without challenges, but the family celebrated small victories together.

Through patience and creativity, Jim and Judy taught their twins a lifelong skill, transforming chaos into harmony and nurturing independence in their little ones.

Three Exercises To Get Organization Underway

Always frame organization as a game or fun activity. Offer gentle guidance but allow them to make decisions to foster independence and celebrate their efforts with high-fives, stickers, or verbal praise.

1. Toy Sorting Adventure

Objective: Teach categorization and designated storage.

How to Play:

- Provide bins or boxes labeled with pictures (e.g., cars, dolls, building blocks).
- Encourage your child to "rescue" toys from the floor and "take them home" to the proper bin.
- Use prompts like, "Where do the cars go?" or "Can you find all the blue blocks?"

Benefits: Develops sorting and classification skills while making cleanup fun.

2. Daily Checklist Chart

Objective: Teach task management and accountability.

How to Play:

- Create a simple chart with pictures or stickers representing daily tasks, such as:
    - Make the bed.
    - Put away toys.
    - Place dirty clothes in the laundry basket.
- Let your child place stickers or draw stars next to completed tasks.

Benefits: Encourages a sense of achievement and introduces the concept of routine and responsibility.

3. Book Sorting Librarian Game

Objective: Keep books organized and accessible.

How to Play:

- Pretend they are a "librarian" organizing a library.
- Teach them to sort books by size, color, or favorite category

(e.g., bedtime stories, animal books).
- Encourage them to neatly stack books on shelves or place them in specific bins.

Benefits: Builds sorting skills and teaches the value of maintaining an orderly space for learning materials. By incorporating these exercises into daily routines, your child will enjoy organizing their space and developing skills that will serve them throughout their lives.

> If you want your children to turn out well, spend twice as much time with them and half as much money.

— Abigail Van Buren, "Dear Abby" newspaper column

Teaching organizational skills is valuable for investing time in a child's growth without material dependence.

Psychology Recognizes The Value of Teaching Kids Organization

Here are a couple of articles discussing why and how young children should learn organization, along with their links for further reading:

5 Ways to Develop Your Child's Organizational Skills[5]

This article offers practical advice on instilling organization in young children, such as using planners, setting routines, and encouraging personal collections to teach categorization and responsibility.

5 Incredible Benefits of Teaching Organization at a Young Age[6]

5. https://www.scholastic.com/parents/family-life/social-emotional-learning/social-skills-for-kids/12-ways-to-develop-your-childs-organizational-skills.html
6. https://www.imagineitdoneny.com/post/teaching-children-organization

This guide discusses the lifelong benefits of teaching organizational habits early, highlighting how these skills improve academic performance and reduce stress.

Long-Term Benefits for Kids

Learning organization at an early age has lasting benefits. Children who grow up with these habits are more likely to excel in school, as they are better equipped to manage their time and assignments. They also tend to experience less stress and anxiety, as an orderly environment can create a calming effect. Moreover, they grow into adults who effectively balance personal and professional responsibilities and recreation.

35. Develop Your Bible Proverbs Method Exercises

Figure 16. Bible Proverbs Method exercise development

Create your, or as a caregiver, someone's personalized exercises with the *Bible Proverbs Method*.

Download this exercise development spreadsheet[1], including about 100 character traits and related Proverbs, to get you started on your journey to lower anxiety and increase mental health with this balanced, Godly Way of progressing.

Your collaborative help and participation are always welcome as we build up more and more precise exercises to help people face and overcome their anxiety, stress, and addictions and reach a balanced, more stable state of mind.

Remember, this prevention method is vital for parents who are preparing the next generation of adults. Focusing on bringing up

1. https://TheExplanation.com/bpmexercisedev

anxiety-freer children is the number one priority to develop a saner society.

Here are the steps to study and develop *Bible Proverbs Method* weekly Exercises.

1. Start with introspection, thinking about your character, personality, and skills, including strengths and weaknesses. Use the list of positive and negative qualities below to help you analyze.
    - Healing: Yourself and others in need.
        i. Know yourself via introspection, meditation, and thinking.
        ii. If you're so inclined, pray and study the Bible about your character.
        iii. Talk with people you're close to and discuss these matters.
    - Nurturing: Those responsible for others: Parents, Teachers, Employers, Managers...
        i. Evaluate others' needs, lacks...
        ii. See where and how you can edify, build up, add value, guide...
2. Find a Proverb related to your specific subject; most will be general.
    - The Proverb should match one of the five traits of consciousness: Reasoning, Purpose, Conduct, Socialization, and Rulership.
    - Drill down to a specific point where you can develop a practical, applicable exercise(s) to work on for one week.
3. Do a Bible Study searching for these qualities, keywords, phrases, and synonyms at UnlockBibleMeaning.com[2]. Draw

2. https://unlockbiblemeaning.com/

out principles and lessons.

4. Find Bible examples of people who had these qualities or did these actions, both good and bad.
    - Ask Google or AI for examples.
5. Find good and bad real-life examples.
    - Ask Google or AI for examples.
6. Find psychological examples and principles. I'm not recommending any websites; these are examples. Use discernment:
    - https://www.psychologytoday.com
    - https://psychcentral.com/
    - https://www.verywellmind.com/
    - https://www.psypost.org/
7. Find inspiring quotes:
    - https://www.brainyquote.com/
    - https://www.azquotes.com/
8. Find exercises:
    - Develop them yourself, ask Google or AI.
    - Make them attainable and measurable to track your successful progress.
9. **Download your COMPASS spreadsheet[3] to personalize, track, and measure your mental health growth**:
    - https://TheExplanation.com/compass
    - File > download
10. **Download the list of character qualities with a corresponding Proverb and its consciousness trait[4].** Each quality can be in more than one of the five consciousness traits.

---

3. https://TheExplanation.com/compass

4. https://theexplanation.com/bpmexercisedev

These are examples you can add to and personalize for yourself and those you mentor to do the same for themselves.

On the downloaded spreadsheet[5], note the column headings D-J. Fill these with Bible study and personal introspection. This action is *self-reproach* (positive qualities you possess and negative flaws), the sixth of the seven points of Conduct. Then, create the weekly exercises for the *Bible Proverbs Method.*

Study and Develop Your Exercises for the Bible Proverbs Method

Reasoning			
Answer soft	15:1	Perception	1:2
Contentment	17:22	Pride	17:19
Criticism	17:10	Prudence	14:17
Discernment	10:13	Silent	17:28
Hope	13:12	Study	15:28
Instruction	12:1	Thoughts	12:5
intelligence	12:8	Tranquility	14:30
Knowledge	18:15	Wisdom before works	3:19
Listen	16:20		

17. Bible Proverbs Method: Reasoning Proverbs

5. https://theexplanation.com/bpmexercisedev

Purpose			
Charlatan	13:1	Luxury	11:3
Confidence	3:25-26	Mediocrity	10:4
Debt	22:07	Money vs. wisdom	16:16
Desire	11:23	Overconfidence	29:23
Giving	22:9	Perseverance	4:26
Honesty in business	11:1	Procrastination	6:4
Hunger urges working	16:26	Prosperity	8:18
Income	16:8	Riches	22:4
Kindness, law of	31:26	Sleep	20:13
Lackadaisical	12:27	Trials	17:3
Laziness	18:09	Work ethics	28:19

18. Bible Proverbs Method: Purpose Proverbs

Conduct			
Alcohol (Wine)	20:01	Heart, merry	15:13
Annoy others	11:29	Honor	22:4
Arrogance	6:17	Joy	17:22
Cheerfulness	17:22	Laughter	14:13
Conduct from heart	4:23	Mischief-making	11:2
Correction-accepting	15:31	Ostentation	17:19
Depression	17:22	Perverseness	11:3
Gluttons	23:20	Proverbs, morality of	10:1

19. Bible Proverbs Method: Conduct Proverbs

Socialization			
Advice	12:5	Ingratitude	17:13
Cheating	20:17	Integrity	20:10
Correction-refusing	15:32	Justice	31:09
Determination	4:25	Lying	19:9
Diligence	10:4	Miser	11:24
Disdain	21:13	Overbearing	14:16
Generosity	11:24	Patience	16:32
Greed	28:25	Stingy	28:22
Humility	18:12		

20. Bible Proverbs Method: Socialization Proverbs

Rulership

Age beauty of men	20:29	Hatred	10:12
Age respect for	16:31	Home, peaceful	17:1
Anger and friendship	22:24	Jealousy	27:4
Animals care for	12:10	Kindness	3:3
Backbiter	16:27	Mercy	14:31
Compassion	19:17	Mocking	17:5
Contentiousness	6:26	Parenting	22:6
Discretion	19:11	Pleasure	21:17
Envy	14:30	Sadness	12:25
Fault, overlooking	17:9	Sharing	3:27
Friend false	12:26	Trust	29:25
Friendship	18:24		

21. Bible Proverbs Method: Rulership Proverbs

Add on your qualities and flaws. Or those positive characteristics you want to inculcate in your children or use as a mentor. Start your *Bible Proverbs Method* journey.

Sharing your mental health journey and destination with your family and trusted friends will help them mentor you and be a personal motivation to continue to push forward, one step at a time, over the next weeks and months. Imagine where you'll be in six months, a year from now.

Untangle your mind, and create a better you.

Epilogue

Ancient Keys To Mental Health

Mind Refreshed is the book's final title, which had the working title _Transform Your Mind Upgrade Your Life_. Here's why.

I brainstormed dozens of titles, even using AI, and many are appealing, exciting, and catchy. However, all are taken by websites and books and don't reflect what I felt we needed for this book. Let me tell you the story it narrates, and you tell me what you think of the title.

Mind Refreshed: Why, How, What of Consciousness and Mind

You can't mend a mind if you don't know what a Mind is! The first item to tick off is the revelation of what the *mind* is and, even more fundamentally, what *consciousness* is. The entire book *Mind-Body Problem Solved*[1] is devoted to this subject. The beginning of *Mind*

1. *https://theexplanation.com/mind*

Refreshed is a concise version revealing the Godly Origin of these two spiritual entities, neshama and ruach[2].

In the Preface, I asked 20 questions relating to Genesis 2:7:

> God formed man from the dust of the earth and breathed the breath of life into his nostrils, and man became a living soul.

The Explanation affirmed that you can only know the fullness of consciousness and mind when you answer those questions. Through the first chapters of *Mind Refreshed*, we resolved those queries using Biblical Hebrew to reach the God-intended meaning of consciousness and the mind's why, how, and what.

God gave neshama and ruach to each human who will ever walk the face of Earth. We are all in the image of God[3] thanks to Him implanting a human portion of His Neshama and Ruach in each of us. Coupled with that infrastructure and energy, He gave us the sacred formula of how to make them function so each human, believer or not, can benefit from a sound mind and possess mental health. That's the second part of the workbook *Mind Refreshed* with *Bible Proverbs Nurturing and Healing Method.*

Please understand: You now have the entire program God set in motion for humankind on Earth. Science and Philosophy are still searching for the **what** of consciousness and mind. Psychology and alternative therapies are tinkering with the **how** of consciousness and mind. Nobody knows the **why** of consciousness and mind.

The key elements for human functioning are a lost cause, and we wonder why we have so much mental illness.

---

2. https://theexplanation.com/2-spirits-neshama-ruach-reveal-human-essence/

3. https://theexplanation.com/gods-plan-story-of-humankind-unbelievable-saga/

We don't need to be ignorant any longer. *Mind Refreshed* reveals the Why, How, and What of Consciousness and Mind and how to Nurture, Heal, and Empower Mental Health. The approach takes the theoretical knowledge all the way to the practical application for all human beings. It's a complete, coherent program.

The Title *Mind Refreshed* Reveals The Bible-Base For Mental Health

Search for *refreshed* at UnlockBibleMeaning.com[4]. Read and meditate on all ten verses and ask yourself, "*Would I like to possess this rest?*" I daresay YES.

Now, switch to Strong's (box on the right), and let's study the God-intended meaning of *refreshed*.

Job 32:20

I [Elihu] will speak, that I may be refreshed (H7304): I will open my lips and answer.

Elihu, the youngest of Job's four friends, was frustrated by the three others' replies to Job. He'd bottled up his speech because of his age. Now, he burst forth with the correct answer to Job's woes and was refreshed. Look at the Biblical Hebrew meaning, especially its origin.

H7304

רָוַח râvach raw-vakh'; a primitive root (identical with H7306 (רוּחַ)); properly, to breathe freely, i.e. revive; by implication, to have ample room:

KJV - be refreshed, large.

4. https://unlockbiblemeaning.com

H7306

רוּחַ rûwach roo'-akh; a primitive root; properly, to blow, i.e. breathe; only (literally) to smell or (by implication, perceive (figuratively, to anticipate, enjoy):

KJV - accept, smell, × touch, **make of quick understanding**.

H7307

רוּחַ rûwach roo'-akh; from H7306 (רוּחַ); wind; by resemblance breath, i.e. a sensible (or even violent) exhalation; figuratively, life, anger, unsubstantiality; by extension, a region of the sky; by resemblance spirit, but only of a rational being (including its expression and functions):

KJV - air, anger, blast, breath, × cool, courage, **mind**, × quarter, × side, spirit(-ual), tempest, × vain, (whirl-) wind(-y).

The origin of *refreshed* is *make of quick understanding* (H7306), and it's precisely the same word in Hebrew as *mind* (H7307). We can say *Mind Refreshed* is: רוּחַ רָוַח (H7307 H7304, Hebrew reads from right to left). Do you see the relationship?

Exodus 23:12

Six days you shall do your work, and on the seventh day you shall rest: that your ox and your ass may rest, and the son of your handmaid, and the stranger, may be *refreshed* (H5314).

The seventh day Sabbath is a *day of refreshing*. People tend to emphasize PHYSICAL rest, which is necessary, but the key is refreshing the whole person, especially their mind. Look at this second Hebrew word translated *refreshed*.

H5314

נָפַשׁ nâphash naw-fash'; a primitive root; to breathe; passively, to be breathed upon, i.e. (figuratively) refreshed (as if by a current of air):

KJV - (be) refresh selves (-ed).

Naphash is the same word as *nephesh* (H5315), *soul,* in Genesis 2:7. The Sabbath is the day for refreshing the soul, which includes the body, consciousness, and mind[5]. We can say *Soul Refreshed* is: נֶפֶשׁ נָפַשׁ (H3515 H3514)

Mind Refreshed: Summary of God's Plan for Humanity

When we come to the Greek New Testament, we also find *Mind Refreshed*. In fact, God's Plan for humankind can be summed up as, "Let this mind be in you, which was also in Christ Jesus" (Philippians 2:5). Paul refers to a *refreshed* or *rested* mind.

1 Corinthians 16:18

For they [messengers from Corinth] have *refreshed* (G373) my spirit (G4151 *pneuma*, the equivalent of *ruach* - mind) and yours: therefore acknowledge you that are such:

G373

5. https://theexplanation.com/bible-ruach-decoded-psychology-mental-activity/

> ἀναπαύω anapauō an-ap-ow'-o; From G303 and G3973; (reflexively) to repose (literally or figuratively (be exempt) remain); by implication to refresh:
>
> KJV - take ease, refresh, (give take) rest.

Rest ties into the Sabbath day of rest, the day for physical rest to refresh the mind and focus it on the mind of Christ.

> **Matthew 11:28**
>
> Come to me, all you that labour and are heavy *laden* (G5412), and I will give you *rest* (G373).

Check *G5412;* Strong refers to it as spiritual anxiety. It includes ***mental anxiety*** that we all suffer from to a more or lesser degree, whether we are believers or non-believers. The remedy is Christ's ***rest***, refreshing ourselves with Christ's spiritual or secular way of life.

The way to have your Mind Refreshed is through the Bible Proverbs Method, which heals mental anxiety and nurtures mental health in our younger generation; this is biblical psychology based on a solid scriptural foundation of understanding the nature of consciousness and mind, how they function, and the formula God gave humankind so each of us possesses a thriving mind.

Mind Refreshed is an apt title for this book that reveals the way to nurture the minds of our younger generation while abetting mental ill-health for the afflicted. It's time to ingrain and share the true story of consciousness and mind along with the how-to approach, the *Bible Proverbs Method*, to change the course of mental health for those closest to you and all people worldwide.

Request for a Book Review

I want to express my gratitude for reading *Mind Refreshed*. An honest review would mean a lot to me, and I would greatly appreciate it if you could take a moment to jot down your thoughts on a couple (or more) of the following points:

- I bought/picked up/received a review copy of this book because….
- Why it interests me, and the audience it would be of use to…
- What I discovered, learned, realized…..
- The changes it has made in my thinking/actions….
- Do you think the author has the right experience and credentials?
- Did the book live up to its description or stated goal?
- Do you recommend it, why?

I appreciate your help in assisting readers to discover this book. Access information for reviews via the link or the QR code below.

https://theexplanation.com/review-mr

Index

Scripture Index - Old Testament

Scripture Index - New Testament

Strong's Index - Hebrews

Strong's Index - Greek

List of Figures

Join *The Explanation News*
Latest blog post notifications and information about *The Explanation*.

https://theexplanation.com/subscribe/

*****

Join the free mini-course
Uncover the Mystery of Adam and Eve's Nakedness
Reach the God-intended meaning of Scripture.

https://TheExplanation.com/naked

Did you love *Mind-Body Problem Solved*? Then you should read *Origin of the Universe* by Sam Kneller!

What is the *Origin of the Universe?* And the fight is on. In the red corner, Science. In the blue corner, Religion. For hundreds of years, the scuffling continues, and there's no clear winner. Now, there is, and it's neither!

Think. The *Origin of the Universe* can only have ONE explanation. To reach that, we must show coherent completeness between Science and God.

Your faith in Science and God hangs in the balance. You can't have confidence in the Big Bang and Creation if you think they are conflicting stories.

Meet the mediator and winner: Theology.

Origin of the Universe makes sense of the Creation story in Genesis 1 and the Big Bang. Based on The *7 Keys to Master Biblical Hebrew*, a Bible study method used by thousands, Sam will help you unlock Bible meaning. You'll have sound evidence that God's Word and scientific facts are coherent, WHY there's confusion, and how to resolve it. That's true theology.

Sheli said, "It is something I have been searching for, a way to get past the translations and get to the deeper meaning of God's word."

Whether you're an unbeliever, novice, or knowledgeable Bible or

Science enthusiast, there's a wealth of wisdom at your fingertips. Each page of *Origin of the Universe* will enhance your insight and become a reference you'll refer to often when studying the Bible and Science.

Buy the e-book or paperback at your favorite online store for a foray into Scripture and Science.

Also by Sam Kneller

The Explanation
Commentary on Genesis 1-3 based on Biblical Hebrew
Inventory of the Universe
Audit of the Universe
Audit of Humankind
Origin of the Universe
Origin of Humankind
Origin of Woman
Agony of Humankind and the Antidote

Essential Bible Basics
Evidence for Bible Wisdom
7 Keys to Master Biblical Hebrew

Mind
Mind-Body Problem Solved
Mind Refreshed

About the Author

After spending twenty-five years in the Christian ministry, Sam Kneller taught at the American University in Paris, was a technical writer, and founded BonjourLaFrance.com, a successful site for travel and tourism in France.

Sam assists truth seekers overcome Bible turbulence and unlock the original God-intended meaning of Scripture via *7 Keys to Master Biblical Hebrew, with no fuss*.

He is the author of the 7-book series *The Explanation*, a commentary on Genesis 1-3 based on Biblical Hebrew. Find Christ and see His amazing role in these chapters on creation.

He teaches and writes about God's Plan and the big questions in life at *https://TheExplanation.com*.

The mission of *The Explanation* is to make accessible the God-intended meaning, in Scripture, of His plan and way of life to believers and non-believers.

Applying Bible benefits transforms into a saner, purposeful life here and now and eternal life in the future.